BITTER

— OR —

BETTER

BITTER
— OR —
BETTER

Crushing Life's
Losses Into Victories

TOM SUTTER

Bitter or Better
Crushing Life's Losses Into Victories
Tom Sutter

www.BitterOrBetterBook.com
tom@BitterOrBetterBook.com

ISBN: 978-0-9908994-0-2 (Trade Paperback)
ISBN: 978-0-9908994-1-9 (mobi eBook)
ISBN: 978-0-9908994-2-6 (epub eBook)

Printed in the United States of America.

*This book is in honor of all the families
who have ever lost a child – may you find the
strength to carry on and overcome any obstacles
life places in your path.*

CONTENTS

Contents

ACKNOWLEDGMENTS

First, and most importantly, I am grateful for my beautiful wife Stacey who was understanding beyond the norm. She put up with my crazy schedule of working the insurance business while co-heading our pediatric cancer charity during most waking hours, seven days a week and then slotting in hundreds of extra hours over the last two years to write this book. Thank you for taking care of everything, I simply ran out of time to handle it all baby!

In second place are our kids – all six of them. Thanks for understanding the craziness that comes along with writing a book. I am proud of each one of you for all that you have become and are going to accomplish in life.

Thank you to everyone who pushed me to write this book especially my buddy Lasse Ingebretsen who made the final, most aggressive push that moved me to action.

Special thanks go to my ghost writer who said I could leave any mention of him out of the book or simply refer to him as a ghost writer. Well, I'm not – Mike Murschel, who is also a Christian counselor, did an awesome job pulling all of this information out of me during our weekly meetings over the first 12 months of the project. Nothing like having great therapy sessions while writing a book!

I owe a debt of gratitude to all of those who took the time out of their busy lives to read the third version of this book, offer feedback, provide testimonials and help me create a richer, more deeply impactful version that will serve as a guide to assist those who are facing one form of adversity or another.

When I was at a loss for the book cover design, I put it out there and asked for help. The father of one of Cal's Angels wish recipients, whose family has become good friends of ours, answered the call. Ryan Felde's suggestions inspired what you see today – Thanks Ryan!

My coach and friend Dave "The Shef" Sheffield who pushed me along the way and wouldn't let me give up or accept the "status quo" when it came to the end result. Then, especially, for making sure the book was ready enough for presales at a major event – thanks brothuh from anothuh mothuh!

Who can forget one's editors – the editing team at Marketing Well Done that included Natasa Zoubouridis, Alec Robbins, Jeremy Caplan, and Kyle Blevons with Collin Henderson taking the lead, took what I believe was going to be a good seller and turned it into what I hope becomes a best seller that positively impacts thousands of lives. You now can confidently add editing to the list of services you provide – awesome job!

Thank you to everyone who is mentioned in the book one way or another. Good, bad or indifferent, I wouldn't be who I am today if it weren't for all of you being in my life.

PREFACE

"Win dis ting!"

Ozzie Guillen before the start
of the first White Sox 2005 playoff game

How many of you have ever been to a major league baseball game? I'm talking MLB, stadium full of cheering fans, music blaring over the loud speakers, emotions raging, competition at its best type of game? And how many of you have ever walked out onto a major league ball field?

I did.

I remember it like it was yesterday — I walked through the underground walkways, came out through the seating area and entered the field through the gates that opened up behind home plate at US Cellular Field, home of the 2005 World Series-winning Chicago White Sox.

But I wasn't carrying a mitt or a ball nor was there a crowd, music or even players . . . the air was cold, the breeze was calm, the sky was grey and the stadium looked larger than life, but yet it was so eerily quiet as I carried the box that contained the ashes of my 13-year-old son Cal on that November day in 2006.

I was with my wife Stacey, Cal's stepmom, Cal's brother Ryan who was 11 at the time, nine-year-old sister Jessie, nine-year-old stepbrother Jason, six-year-old stepsister Kiley and eight-month-old half-sister Lexie — little Ellie who was born in 2008 was only a distant thought at that time.

We were there to fulfill one of the wishes Cal expressed as he was dying just three months earlier. Not a conversation you ever want to have with your child nor even a conversation you can imagine having in your worst of nightmares but, as the cancer was sucking the life out of him, Cal had the wherewithal to give me a laundry list of places he would like us to place his ashes and the pitcher's mound at the home of his favorite team was one of them.

As we walked onto the field I was holding the box on the underside of my forearm like I used to carry him as a baby — head in my palm and his little baby butt in the nook of my elbow ... the box fit right in that same space just like he did 13 years earlier ...

Four Standing Taller Than Others Left to Right — Tom, Kiley, Ryan and Jessie. Front and Lower Left to Right — Stacey, Lexie, Jason and Ellie.

This one goes down in the annals of all time hard conversations.

Several years ago I was at a former client's office cleaning up a slight mess caused by an assistant who forgot to complete some paperwork. Not a big deal; I was able to fix it before there was a real problem like an uncovered claim or something along those lines. The cost of the fix was an additional $500 which really irritated my client. Not sure if it was with me, his assistant or the insurance company, but from his actions it was quite clear he was pissed. He went on and on and on about how it could have put him out of business, $500 is a lot of money, sh.. this, g damn that, can't people follow simple directions, who's covering the $500 and so on.

Finally, about five minutes into his rant I said it just like it is written so as not to agitate him but show I was in shock "Daaaang, you just keep going on like someone died. Let me ask you one question — Are your kids still alive and healthy?"

You could see the instant look of shock on his face as he paused, thought about what he was going to say, looked straight at me and said with an air of surprise in his voice, "You aren't going to pull that one on me, are you?"

I quickly interjected so that he couldn't misinterpret the intent and said, "You should have heard yourself. I didn't even know who you were there nor did I want to like you. It was easily five minutes and you were still rolling so I had to interject with a shocking statement to make you stop."

Not wanting him to cut in until I was done I kept talking, "In the scheme of things, is it really a big deal? Based on your revenues, $500 is a very small percentage and price to pay for a learning lesson. There are much bigger issues at hand to concern yourself with than this."

He paused, looked around for a bit and couldn't help but have the last word, which I knew he would, and said half smiling, "I understand but still I'm pissed that you took away every reason for me to be upset." We finished business and I sat wondering whether my comments would strain our relationship. He did call a week or so later and thanked me for the reality check but added that he was still pissed I did it. I asked him if he was really pissed that I said it and he laughed while saying, "Yeah, I like venting every once in a while, but now every time I start, I think about what you said and I just can't get very upset after all … you bastard."

That's his way of thanking me for the reality check while still showing he's tough — I know I hit a nerve, but outwardly letting me know it would show vulnerability; not very masculine in his book.

I have had some hard conversations with folks who have had similar experiences to mine, especially those who have lost a child as this single event can ruin someone's life by causing them to simply give up. The way I see it, I can have these conversations because I have lived through their ordeal and know within a margin of error of less than 1% what they're thinking and feeling and what they want to say. I wish I didn't, but I do and since I do, I may as well help them through it so that they don't make choices like I have seen so many others do.

An example of this is a dad who lost his oldest child, who had nothing but what would seem to be a great life ahead of him. When he finally went back to work he and I spoke and he told me that he was really struggling with doing anything more than routine tasks that took little to no effort. He said that as soon as he had to put more than simple routine thought into anything he felt like giving up, quitting his job and curling up in a ball.

Yes, I know exactly how he feels as I still feel this way at times and probably will for the rest of my life. The thought of your child no longer being here, no longer coming home from school, going out with his buddies, playing catch with you in the backyard or sitting down to a meal at the dinner table with the rest of the family is overwhelming. If you let it creep in, it will consume you and control your actions, even resulting in complacency and inaction. It takes a conscious effort to thwart the attack and in this case I offered up some hard talk that I hope hit home as it is what I use to conquer the thought demons that are trying to cause me to give up and fail.

Of course, I asked first if I could offer up some hard talk and he said he needs something. I started right in by saying, "Don't be selfish. If you give up now you're only thinking of yourself and you cannot do that. You have to think about your wife and other kids. You have to think about your employer and co-workers. You have to step outside yourself and think of others first and what negative impact you will have on everyone's life if you give up."

There was silence and he hesitantly said, "Okay," as if it was a question rather than an agreement. I knew he needed more clarification so I continued.

"You hold a very high level job where a lot of people depend on your success in completing the task correctly and efficiently. If you give up and lose your clients, you will lose your job and your family will suffer. If a big enough chunk of revenue goes away, some or all of those on your team will lose their jobs. Some of those that lose their jobs have kids in college that they will no longer be able to afford. Some won't be able to take a much needed vacation. Customers may end up doing business with second rate providers and their businesses will suffer. It's a trickle down reaching way beyond just you, my friend."

He admitted that he never thought of it this way and was shocked by the amount of other people's fate he held in his hands. He thanked me and we hung up.

About a week later we spoke again and he said that he had drummed up conversations with those he knows depend on his performance. He was shocked to actually learn how far reaching the consequences would be if he were to simply give up. Not only would some miss out on vacations and not be able to afford college, but he went on to add that if any of his team's kids had to drop out of college, they might end up working at a low paying job the rest of their life rather than becoming an attorney, a doctor or stock broker. Their lost hopes and dreams would be on his shoulders.

A chain reaction like this may seem a little far-fetched and whether it is or not, thoughts like this have allowed him to redirect his focus from only thinking about himself to thinking about what ramifications his actions, or inactions, will have on others. While I am not a licensed psychologist or therapist, I have been asked for advice on how I "do it." As long as they're open to some "hard talk," I cut to the chase and tell them to stop being selfish by wanting to give up. That's where the conversation begins; where it goes depends on whether they're just saying they want to change or if they really do want to change.

The strength and courage Cal showed throughout his battle with cancer is what pushed us to do something with the tragedy we just experienced and start Cal's All-Star Angel Foundation — a 501c3 nonprofit pediatric cancer organization created in his memory. Wise beyond his years and maybe even unbeknownst to him, Cal cared about others before he even thought about himself, which is what keeps us on our path to running Cal's Angels with others in mind before ourselves. Our main mission and purpose of granting the wishes of kids fighting cancer and financially assisting their families continues Cal's legacy and it is the real life stories of the battles against cancer of all the families we help that keep us persevering through what at times seem to be insurmountable obstacles.

It is also the stories like that of Cal's brother who was ten at the time and knew no better that are real eye openers. After watching Cal get every cool electronic device on the street, he made the off-the-cuff comment that he wished one day he got cancer so that he could get the same or better. This one single personal experience is the major reason why we make it a point to also take care of the siblings of these brave little cancer fighters.

And because of my passion for the overarching mission of helping other families through their battles with pediatric cancer, 10% of all proceeds from this book are going right into the foundation that bears my oldest boy's name —

Visit us at www.calangels.org to learn about all that we do for the families whose struggles we know all too well. While you're there, check out our upcoming events — we'd love to have you join us!

FOREWORD

Tony Rubleski

A s a writer and professional speaker I'm on the road a lot. It's a unique lifestyle and requires flexibility, patience, and in my opinion a good sense of humor. The time spent in airports, in different cities, and with many new people entering the daily parade can be viewed as either stressful or an interesting adventure. I view it as not just a job, but a rewarding adventure.

In my many travels I'm fortunate and blessed to meet great people. Some are more memorable than others, while a few change my outlook about life in a deeply profound and unexpected way. Tom Sutter is one such person who has had this positive impact on my life.

We met in April of 2013 at an event I was hosting in Del Mar, California. On day one of the event, one of our speakers, Tom Cunningham, called him out from the audience and up on stage to briefly explain his charity and the story behind it. As Tom Sutter nervously grabbed the microphone and began to tell the story of his son Cal and his death at age 14 from cancer and the charity he started to honor him, I stopped what I was doing and listened intently. To say that I was touched by Tom's message is a massive understatement.

After the event Tom and I stayed in touch and I became not only hooked on Tom's vision of service to others, but more importantly with the incredible services Cal's All-Star Angel Foundation provides for hundreds of children and the families who cope with not just a cancer diagnosis, but also the many new challenges and stresses it produces. To put a smile on not just the face of a child battling cancer, but also the families and caretakers as well, is beautiful to witness and see in action. It also serves as a positive reminder as to how truly caring and loving we humans can be to our fellow brothers and sisters in times of crisis and intense stress.

This past March I had a chance to attend the annual dinner gala and major fundraiser to benefit Cal's Angels in Chicago. This was one of those special nights in my life. As I left the event for my 3-hour drive back to Michigan, I couldn't get over not just the outpouring of generosity from the 600+ attendees, but also meeting and hearing many of the children, parents, siblings, sponsors and volunteers share how the Foundation has positively impacted them. This left a very positive impression on my soul that to this day has changed my view on life, but also as to how I look at my role as a post-divorce father and the relationship I have with my own three children.

As I finished reading the manuscript a second time for the book you now hold in your hand, I couldn't help but flash back to the similarities of Tom's journey and those of another father who turned the tragic loss of his son into a positive movement for good and service to mankind. His name is John Walsh. I met him at an event we spoke at together back in 2005 and noted that Walsh turned his own tragedy into a massive force for good when his son Adam was abducted in 1981 at a shopping mall in south Florida. Not only is he most known for his long-running TV show, *America's Most Wanted,* but he will also go down in the pages of history as the central force and advocate for the present day Amber alert system.

John's relentless drive and persistence has saved children, helped law enforcement solve countless crimes, and take dangerous predators and thugs off the streets. It wasn't an easy mission as he encountered heavy resistance from the status quo and many within Congress who believed that law enforcement and the way things were being done was just fine. Walsh would not be stopped. Eventually his hard work and tenacity was recognized by the President of the United States, with many new changes in law enforcement procedures and new laws put into place in his son's name as the reward for his tireless efforts.

I view Tom and John's journey in many similar ways. Tom didn't have a say in his son contracting cancer, nor did John Walsh ever fathom that on a trip to the store in 1981 his son would disappear, never to be seen again. The reason for both life events happening will never be known. However, each man did have a huge choice on how they'd let these events impact their lives after their sons were gone. In that process, they both followed their hearts, but also their inner intuition, when fear and possible self-sabotage could have easily stopped most others.

Tom decided he'd turn his bitterness and loss into something better. The memory of his son Cal could be used as a dynamic force for good in a way that would stay true to Cal's influence on others when we was still living.

> *"Experience: that most brutal of teachers.*
> *But you learn, my God do you learn."*
>
> – C.S. Lewis

Tom's journey has been full of adversity and he doesn't sugarcoat or pretend to be perfect within the pages of this book. He's human like the rest of us, but his heart and passion to serve others is far beyond what he ever imagined might be possible. While Cal is not with us in physical form today, his spirit of love and compassion live on daily through the work of his father Tom, his step-mom, his brothers and sisters and the countless other earthly angels that still reside today in helping bring joy and compassion to those going through a rough patch on this trip called life.

Thank you again Tom for all you do and especially for taking the time from an already jam-packed life to capture your wisdom and stories for others to gain from within the pages of this inspiring book.

Tony Rubleski
President, Mind Capture Group

"This book will make you laugh, make you cry, and inspire you-all at the same time. Tom pulls back the curtain on how he transformed himself personally, professionally, and also how he turned an unimaginable tragedy into an amazing foundation that touches the lives of thousands of people every year."

– Dave "The Shef" Sheffield
Top Requested Motivational Speaker and Author

"I think about Tom Sutter a lot. Mostly, when I look at my wife- someone who's dealt with chronic, debilitating health issues as long as I've known her. I can't even imagine her health deteriorating to the point where I lost her. It's too much. Hell, my dog turns 9 years old soon, and the thought of losing her destroys me. How could I ever bear the hurt of losing a child?

And that's often when I think of Tom. How does he not only carry on, but thrive? How is he able to stay so close to the very thing that took his boy? Why isn't he angry? Why isn't he selfish?

If you know Tom, well, the answer is pretty clear. Because he's a man of character; he's a man who refuses to lie down; and he's a man who refuses to let others go through what he and his family did, and not try to help them.

That's what Tom Sutter is. This book details the why and the how. Much like Cal's Angels started in his living room with a handful of people, Tom's personal journey to the man he is now had humble beginnings, and was born of struggle. But also like Cal's, it's a success story, and a lesson to anyone who's been knocked flat by life.

You can get back up again."

– Pat Tomasulo
Sports Anchor and Reporter for WGN-TV Chicago

"I have had the distinct opportunity and pleasure of working with Tom Sutter on the Board of Directors for Cal's Angels for more than a year. In that time, I have come to know a man who has turned the tragic loss of his eldest son, Cal, into a foundation that helps so many young kids battling cancer, as well as their siblings. In a few short years Cal's Angels has become an incredible foundation grown from his love for Cal.

Tom is relentless in his quest to grow Cal's into a large foundation while still holding true to the core beliefs of its founding, and that is what sets him *well above other business leaders that I have worked with, and sets Cal's well above other charitable causes.*

Since serving on the Board of Directors for Cal's I have learned many things from Tom, not the least of which is how to turn strong business leadership skills into something so much bigger than one's self. I have witnessed how Tom uses those skills to motivate a diverse set of people into a cause so worthy, and for that, I am eternally grateful.

Better or Bitter takes you through Tom's life and its many twists and turns. With each, is a lesson or two to be learned about faith, perseverance, struggle, tragedy and triumph…about life. While Tom articulates how that has helped him in his career in business, what is clear is that these experiences are what drives his passion for, and the mission of Cal's Angels.

The lessons in this book are relevant for readers from all walks of life as we are each presented with challenges in so many different ways."

– Keith D. Olinger
Senior Director, Microsoft Corporation
Director, Board of Directors, Cal's Angels

"I am a fairly ferocious reader so I have absolute respect for anyone that can take the time to write a book about himself with really no filter or worry of consequence. You left no stone unturned. Toward the end I was thinking to myself all he needs to do is talk about politics and you will have hit every sensitive topic and then there it was around chapter 16 or 17 you made mention of politics."

– Brian Pascoe
President, Illinois/Wisconsin Region, Verizon Wireless

"I've known Tom since our undergraduate days at 'the Harvard of the Midwest' NIU and the Sigma Chi fraternity. Some worked hard scholastically, while others took advantage of extracurricular activities that a fraternity and Midwest college have to offer. I'd put Tom and I in the latter category. If you had to put an over/under on whether Tom would rise above the tragedy of losing a child and contribute to others in a meaningful way as a result, I would have taken the under and doubled up! Tom and Stacey's vision and tireless activities have provided innumerous opportunities to benefit families; from scholarships to pizza parties while receiving treatment to assisting

families with medical bills. Sometimes it's just a shoulder to cry on or a voice that has gone through it to help..."

– Robert Dahl, MBA, SVP, COO

"As someone who has also suffered a tragic loss in their life, losing my son in a terrible accident, I know how hard it can be to recover from such a devastating blow. The old cliché that "your children are not supposed to die before you" doesn't come close to describing the amount of pain a parent experiences when a tragedy like this does occur.

I have known Tom for almost 15 years, both professionally and personally, and watched him navigate the perilous journey on which Cal's disease took them. It is a testament to Tom's strength of character that he has been able to create so much good and goodness from Cal's battle against cancer. From the amazing, wonderful accomplishments of the non-profit organization he created, Cal's Angels, to this book "Bitter or Better," Tom provides a blueprint for taking the tragedies and hardships that may find their way into our lives and turning them into an affirmation of love and life, and thoughtful remembrances of all the loved ones who share, and have shared, our life."

– Glenn Brown
CEO/CFO, Gane Brothers & Lane (NCALA, LLC)

"I came to know Tom Sutter, and his wife Stacey, through his leadership of Cal's All Star Angel Foundation (Cal's Angels), which has benefitted the lives of hundreds of families since its inception.   Until reading this book, though, I had not realized the many agonizing "shocks to the system" that he had experienced as a child and young adult.   And, then, while thriving in his thirties--with a successful second marriage and career--Tom faced the greatest shock of his life: the death of his oldest child Cal. Tom could have run away or given up. He had, after all, faced more tragedy than many of us ever encounter. He could have retreated and rested in the solace on his other children and wife. Instead, he chose a different path.

Buttressed by his trust in God and the love of his family and friends, he started Cal's Angels.   Tom truly lives with a "passion-infused purpose" and this purpose fuels Cal's Angels. It has spread to the many volunteers and donors who are involved with Cal's Angels. I have the greatest admiration for Tom--for the obstacles he has overcome, his depth of commitment, the focus of his mission, and the impact he has had on so many."

– Rev. Donald J. Camp

"This is the kind of story - of both tragedy and triumph - of the human spirit that will touch your heart and soul. Tom's story holds nothing back and his vulnerability in every step of his journey is both rare and priceless. His authenticity will soothe you no matter what you may have experienced or are presently experiencing. It doesn't matter whether this book touches the heart of every reader or a single reader, as the value of a single life cannot be quantified in both what each of us is during our time on earth, and what each of us can do with what time is left to affect others."

– Mike Muhney, Software Entrepreneur
(Co-Inventor of ACT! for Windows and Inventor of
VIPorbit for Apple devices for Relationship Management)

*"**Bitter or Better** is a poignant look on how a man takes on incredible life challenges as a child, father, and husband. Tom deals with struggles that most of us will never have to endure. From childhood pain, to a run in with the law, then the biggest heartbreaker, losing his oldest son to leukemia… what does one do with so much bitter in their life? Instead of wallowing in self pity, Tom and his wife, Stacey, set out to make the lives of other children who are fighting childhood cancer a little better through their organization, Cal's All-Star Angel Foundation. Faced with the same adversity, many people would choose the bitter route, but Tom rises above the pain to become a better man."*

– Taksina Davis

"On the surface, Tom Sutter's life appears to be all about his son Cal dying at the age of 13 due to childhood leukemia. His book will help you think, speak and act differently about a variety of other challenges that Tom has faced along the way, just as you and I do in some form or fashion.

Tom speaks openly about some of his invisible challenges that have shaped him - things like mental and physical abuse, bullying, parenthood, marriage and God.

His life experience has helped him discover his, and Cal's, God given Definite Purpose and it will impact people from all walks of life including you."

– Tom too tall Cunningham

INTRODUCTION

I started out writing this book centered on the biggest tragedy of my life which was losing my 13-year-old son, Cal, to leukemia in August of 2006 and what became of my life after that single event. During the almost two year process of getting everything out there and on paper, I learned a lot about myself, why I am who I am and why I act the way I do. I now know that what I started doing after his death really was a culmination of what I learned through the sometimes unbelievable trials and tribulations I faced in my life.

There were many obstacles put in my path that I had to overcome and adversity beyond what most "normal" people can comprehend as being reality rather than fantasy with some being downright nightmares. The human mind is an intriguingly spectacular thing and what it can accomplish — or not accomplish — is even more amazing.

There was a pre-destined path my life took which I liken to an extended period of basic training for any of the armed services before going head first into war.

Who would have guessed that being bullied both at home in an alcohol fueled atmosphere and amongst your peers contained valuable life lessons you can use to your advantage? Or that becoming a drug and alcohol user, troublemaker and anti-authority figurehead who wound up in jail for fighting would also contain valuable lessons to apply to the rest of your life?

I certainly didn't think of it that way as my life was unfolding one heartache after another. However, that exact path my life took did prepare me for the ultimate test anyone will ever face — their child's agonizing fight with cancer that ultimately claims their life.

Before it all starts, it really is hard to imagine your 12-year-old son, who has never had much more than strep throat, suddenly being diagnosed with the adult form of leukemia as a child.

That is exactly what happened to our oldest child Cal, the oldest in a blended family of seven kids, in June of 2005. It threw our entire family into a tailspin.

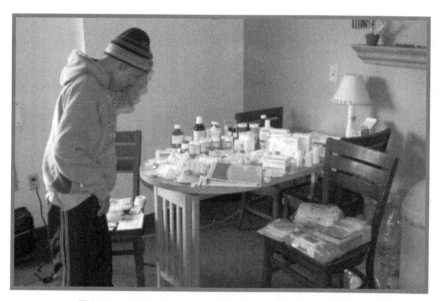

This scene is familiar to any family dealing with cancer.
The supplies and meds have a habit of overtaking the home.

As a parent you want to figure out a way to take this cancer out of your child. If nothing else, take it upon yourself to fight it, but you can't, so you prepare as best you can for a battle that I don't think ever even occurred in my nightmares. But here it was, happening to our family.

What did we all do to deserve this?

How could God do this to such a young boy who was physically fit and an excellent athlete?

Why, why, why?

There is no time to search for these answers during the battle — you have to research all you can, learn the ins and outs of cancer and determine how best to keep the entire family together during this fight. You have a sick child and knowing how cancer seemingly has a mind of its own, you know it could turn on a dime and he could lose this battle.

You also have to be concerned about the other kids and your spouse. They all depend on you as well and while it's understood you have to spend more time with the one who is fighting for his life, they too can feel slighted.

Cal's brother Ryan is a perfect example. As a ten-year-old boy, he saw his older brother getting all these cool gifts — an Xbox 360 when it first came out, iPods, Nintendo DS games, books, games, clothes, money, Yu-Gi-Oh cards, and on and on. Ryan made an off the cuff the comment about how he wished he could get cancer one day so that he could get all this cool stuff too.

Whoa!

Our other kids ranged from a newborn that arrived nine months into Cal's battle to an eight-year-old, so there were as many ways of dealing with the situation as there were people in the family. We made every effort to keep the other kids' lives as normal as possible — they still went to school every day, had play dates and participated in sports. The only difference was that they spent some time with their brother either in the hospital or with him when he was home. It was this normalcy that kept everyone in check.

I had to also make sure I did not forget about my wife, Stacey, Cal's stepmom, during this very trying segment of our lives. We had just been married five months before Cal was diagnosed and I was spending 50% of the time with Cal while he was inpatient for 11 out of 14 ½ months. Stacey and I remained in constant contact while I was with Cal. She was the backbone and support of the family while I was away and I was there for everyone while home. It takes an extra level of communication to keep it all together and an extraordinary level of mental strength to keep you on the right path.

Through an ordeal like this it is very easy to be bitter about everything and towards everyone, including God. You really don't know what to think. Your actions, thoughts, and impulses seem to be on auto-pilot, almost occurring on a whim and under their own power. It takes some deep self-reflection to keep it all in check because one day this will all be over and the "normal life" you left behind will one day be your "new normal life" in which you will have to adapt or change either with or without your child.

It takes a lifetime of preparation and a lot of introspect to go from Bitter to Better which is the exact path we chose.

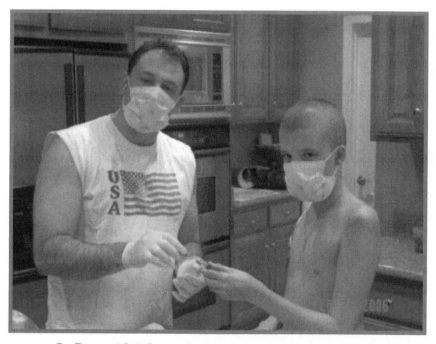

Dr. Tom and Cal. Cancer Dads are sometimes overlooked, but, like Cancer Moms, learn to be de facto med techs to care for their children.

Some people lose everything when something like this occurs. Their jobs are gone, homes foreclosed upon, cars repossessed, families split apart — you name it, it happens and can happen more easily if you let the cancer that is eating away at your child also eat away at you, your thoughts, and your soul. It's a nasty disease that does not discriminate and it can claim its victims anywhere very quickly or very slowly while causing collateral damage beyond anything you can imagine. It can change a person's innermost thoughts, how they act and what they believe. This is exactly what happened to our family during Cal's battle with cancer, and even more so after he passed away in August of 2006.

Cal Sutter #9 — All-Star Pitcher and Center Fielder for the Angels of the South Elgin, Illinois, Little League

WHY THIS BOOK AND WHY NOW?

"Bullying is one of the most prevalent and insidious challenges faced by many people from all walks of life. Whether it be at home, at school, in public or in the workplace, bullying is a nondiscriminatory epidemic that changes its victims' lives forever. A select few wind up for the better, most for the worse, but never leaves them the same at the back end of it all.

The bullying I faced as a child from the outside forces, as well as from within our family unit, shaped who I have evolved into today: From the shy, withdrawn child who refused to talk much, to the outwardly aggressive bully basher who faced the ultimate bully...cancer.

While that bully claimed one of the most important pieces of my life, I refused to let it claim everything. I fought back and refused to lose this fight — this is the one bully who keeps coming back to indiscriminately claim innocent victims, but it could not claim my inner self.

In the battle with a bully you may lose some or even most of the rounds of the fight, get beat up in the process and feel like giving up. I am here to help you understand and truly believe that no matter who the bully is or what shape, form or figment of your imagination it assumes, you can come out on top by refusing to let the bully win. By keeping your head in the game all the way through, even a bully as big, bad and ugly as cancer can be beaten.

Cancer took my son's life, but I absolutely refuse to let it ruin mine, my family's, my friends', or anyone else's I come in contact with in life."

A good friend of mine, Lasse Ingebretsen, is the last one in a chain of individuals responsible for me taking action to write this book. He is the one who succeeded in encouraging me, prompting me and motivating me to bring this project to fruition.

The final "discussion" occurred at an outdoor concert in 2012. He pulled me aside and in a serious tone said, "I know you pretty good; I know your story well — now is the time to write the book many have been encouraging you to write. You cannot keep them waiting any longer."

So here it is — not a book about, "O' woe is me, look what I went through ... please feel sorry for me!" Nor is it a book about making excuses for my "misdeeds" in life.

Rather, it's a book about discovering that no matter what amount of crap life throws at you, there is no reason to give up. You can turn that crap into gold, not so much for yourself, but for others, no matter what walk of life they follow.

It's also a book about parenting and not so much what to do, but what not to do.

As parents, you are role models to your children and they naturally look up to you, wanting to be like you. The environment you create for them at home becomes their "normal" and what they will naturally gravitate towards as adults. Create a chaotic environment and, believe me from first-hand experience, a chaotic environment is what your children will seek out. It will be what makes them feel most comfortable and "at home," so to speak. It will be their "normal."

At some point in their lives, some will realize they need a "new normal", but most will be helplessly stuck in their old "normal" thinking that there is no way out, no way they can change.

But they can, and I am proof of that.

Inside these pages you will find me at my best and at my worst. In this is everything from the baggage of my past, my initial nerdiness, and what turned me into an athlete, at first in control, and then out of control, and how that landed me in jail.

You will find out about my childhood, my failed first marriage, my kids, and my wonderful second wife. You will relive with me the tragedy of my eldest child's death from leukemia and how that could have destroyed me, but instead empowered me to finish the path I started when I met Stacey; a path of going against the grain of anything I had ever done for anyone but myself, and my ultimate decision to provide a not-for-profit foundation designed to help others facing similar life altering moments.

You have to understand that I was not raised to do what I now consider second nature — it was really more the opposite. However, the culmination of events served to bring me to the point I am at today.

Either directly or indirectly, I help a lot of people on a regular basis. I did not think I would ever do things like this. My background, the people I have met and the circumstances that brought me to this point, all these experiences, have given me the unique ability to relate to just about anybody from any background.

From the people who shared that jail experience with me, to leaders in business and academics, to laymen, housewives and students, I know them all inside and out and I want to share what I've learned with you. The material I have stored up over the years needs to come out for the good of everyone. I am bursting at the seams with the need to share and finally am comfortable enough with who I am to do this.

Do I fear that by laying it all out there, especially the bad "stuff," some might think that I really have not changed or believe people can't change, thus taking this in the wrong light and shunning me? Of course, but all I ask is that you look at me now and who I have become on a consistent basis for well over ten years. I feel the extreme need to live by my own Personal Vision Statement which is, "I am going to use my life's experiences to help others overcome adversity and persevere through anything life throws at them, feel good about who they are, and achieve their dreams."

Note that this book does not include every single detail or every single messed up story, circumstance or situation throughout my journey as a lot of it is way beyond what most can understand and/or even comprehend as being reality.

Not to over-simplify it, but if I can do it, anybody can do it to one extent or another, but the key is having the desire and drive to do so.

CHAPTER ZERO

The Story of Cal's Angels

"Success is not to be pursued;
it is to be attracted by the person you become."

Jim Rohn, American Entrepreneur,
Author and Motivational Speaker

The creation of Cal's All-Star Angel Foundation is a story in and of itself.

It goes back to the several years long perfect storm that created a chain of events coming together and inspiring us to create one of the most exciting 501c3 non-profit organizations around. What makes this story so interesting is that volunteerism was never in my blood but rather looked at as something that would hinder my ability to be successful in the business world. I would be asked to volunteer for some great causes but could never get past the thought that putting in less than 70 to 80 hours per week in the insurance business would kill my prospects of making it big. Little did I know that quite the opposite was going to happen and prove to me

1

that thinking of others first really is the best way to lead your life both personally and professionally.

During the 14 ½ months of Cal's fight with cancer, I worked no more than part time at the insurance business. Even though the insurance agency folks were doing a lot more for me than they would under normal circumstances, I quickly realized I didn't need to work much more than that to keep my clients on board and only a little more to have time to pick up new clients. I learned a lot about prioritization, delegation and the importance of team work especially the fact that a great team is what you need to succeed, not just personal gumption. This has carried over into how I have run my life since Cal's passing and subsequently co-founded Cal's Angels. I no longer work more than 40 to 50 hours per week at the insurance gig, or what I refer to as my first job or "the job that pays the bills," but yet my insurance business has doubled while my personal sense of self-worth and satisfaction with life is off the charts. Don't get me wrong, I still work the 70 to 80 hour work weeks it's just that the extra hours go into charity work and here is how what I call my second job or "the job that pays the heart" came to be.

I had always heard of the stories of family struggles during a child's serious illness but they were just that, "stories." I couldn't fathom the reality of people losing their jobs, cars and homes, not being able to put good food on the table, families breaking up, divorce, desertion by one spouse or the other, fighting or any other form of domestic mayhem occurring at the same time their child is battling a serious illness. But there I was, thrust into a situation I did not want to be in nor ever wish upon my worst of enemies. Just by being in that environment I came to know all too well that these stories are true. They are real and they happen to people just like you and me — unwilling participants in a nightmare come true.

Because Cal ultimately lost his battle with cancer, the right word may not be lucky but no other word is a viable substitute when I say we were lucky that none of the "stories" happened to us throughout Cal's battle with cancer. We owe it all to the great people in our lives that were there to support us and prevent us from experiencing any additional heartaches which allowed us to focus more on spending time with Cal. A lesson we would not ever forget and a big part of why we, and especially me, do what we do with Cal's Angels.

One particular story that serves as the impetus for Cal's Angels is the one about Cal's 14-year- old roommate who was an only child. His dad and I were playing Play Station 2 with the boys when the dad said he had to leave asking if his son could still hang out with us. Knowing I could have drawn the curtain I didn't even hesitate when I said "of course he can." The dad proceeded to tell me he had to go to Northwestern because his wife had breast cancer.

Wow! How do I come up with any kind of answer or logical response to that? I was dumbfounded, at a loss for words, all choked up and felt like reaching out to hug this guy whom I really didn't even know.

Before I could do or say anything he told me he had to walk to the shopping mall to get his car. Knowing it was close to two miles away I asked if he knew he could get a special sticker for parking and all it would cost is $2.00 per day. He said he knew that but he lost his job and needs the $2.00 to eat. My heart actually hurt when I heard this, my stomach felt cramped feeling like I was going to puke and all I could muster up to say without losing all composure is, "Let me give you some money" while pulling out my wallet.

He quickly interjected that he was fine and didn't need any money.

When looking at him, yes, you'd think he was fine and no worries in life. He was happy, had a smile on his face, dressed well, was clean shaven and well groomed but I couldn't help but say out loud (only in my head of course), "There's no way you're fine, no possible way you could be at all!"

But the way he looked at me when he said he was fine I knew it would insult him if I pushed on with the offer of help.

He went on his way that late afternoon and we checked out in the morning before I was able to get his contact info. Never did see him again but that night after he left I got the boys in bed then called Stacey to tell her the story. She was as shocked and saddened about it as me and I told her at that moment whether Cal makes it or not, we have to do something for families just like his.

While this is the most impactful story for me and provides the most impetus for how I now lead my life, there are many more that are different and impactful to varying degrees.

On one of our stays in the hospital, we were on the isolation side of the floor where there are two sets of doors you go through before entering the room. One set goes from the hall into a middle room where you scrub down, disinfect and put on protective clothing to keep germs out and the second lets you into the room. In the isolation rooms, the patient is required to stay on the other side of the second door until released — the possibility of exposing a compromised immune system during stem cell transplant or intense therapy is the main concern.

One morning bright and early there was a huge commotion in the room next to Cal's. I could hear a child screaming, doors banging, people yelling and others running down the hall. I poked my head out of the room to see what's up and there was this young boy, maybe eight-years-old, in a gown at the door to the hall pulling on it, screaming, "Where is my mommy? I want my mommy!"

Absolutely heart wrenching but obviously nothing I could do.

I later learned that his mom is a true single mom — no dad or other means of financial support other than her own job so she had to go to work leaving care of her child to the social workers. He obviously wanted no part of that and was going to get out of the room to find his mom all the while nurses and social workers were holding the door shut yelling at him to go back in the room so they could come in. They were trying to reason with an eight-year-old telling him about germs, infection, etc. but it wasn't working.

This went on for at least an hour before he finally calmed down. It was so hard to witness and I felt so awful for that boy and his mom. I just wanted to change and be his mom for at least that moment so I could go in there to be with him but, of course, I couldn't. Instead the visual of the absolutely terrified look in his eyes and gut wrenching, heart breaking sounds of his screams will be forever etched into my memory. This is one of "those stories" I wish I could forget about but I can't so instead it gives me that extra fire to push on and do good things for these kids and their families.

While the story about the dad and only child with leukemia is the most impactful in making me realize these "stories" of heartache and loss are real, the experience I had in witnessing Cal's last breath is the one that gives me strength in anything and everything I do in life.

During his last days all Cal wanted to do was get home to his own bed and see his dog. We were able to secure him a flight on a medical transport jet that got him to the local municipal airport in time to get him to his own bed at his mother's house. I can go on about that two day ordeal but it really is a book in itself. Though she truly and sincerely hates me, his mother was gracious enough to let me spend time with Cal in her home and for that I am forever grateful albeit she made it quite the experience that was never dull.

For instance, one of Cal's last wishes was that he wanted his mom and me to get along. We both told him we would definitely try. However, while Cal was barely clinging to life, she got so worked up about the fact that I took back my long lost painting that she "mistakenly kept" during the divorce, she hid around the corner of the closet door where he couldn't see and mouthed the words "f… that" when I reminded her about Cal's wish.

There were other incidents, but that was the worst instance of the craziness I dealt with while trying to spend time with Cal while he was dying. Nothing I could really do about any of it, I was a guest in her house and had to deal with it.

In hindsight, my experience in dealing with all of "that" has become part of the Cal's Angels story in that it has helped us understand the craziness that occurs within the families battling pediatric cancer. It is this understanding of unforeseen variables impacting the family units we assist that has become integral to our success.

During his last moments, I was lying right next to Cal on his left side with my right arm around him looking at his face — the face that only resembled the vibrant young man Cal grew to be before cancer turned him into a skeletal looking shell of his prior self. His breathing got slower until he took that one last breath. He did not breathe again; he did not move but fell limp. My boy, my first born, my athlete, my first reason for becoming a responsible adult was no longer here with me and I would never hear his sweet voice again except for in my head and in recordings.

I laid there for what seemed like an eternity and cried while holding him with my right arm. I did not want to let go. The mental and emotional pain I felt was excruciating and beyond description. I felt lonely, scared, empty and angry all at once. But yet at the same time there was a hint of relief that his pain and suffering were finally over. He was free from the cancer and on his way to heaven to be with God, Jesus and all of our friends and family members who died before him. He was going to be able to play baseball once again while waiting for the day I join him to play catcher for the best pitcher and centerfielder I have ever known.

Late in the evening the coroner came to get him and when he walked up the long, single flight of stairs to his room I insisted that I carry Cal to the hearse. I gave Cal one last hug and a kiss on the forehead before they covered him up. As I carried him from his room across the landing to the stairs, his lifeless body seemed heavier than it had ever been at any point in his life.

Before those last few days, the last time I walked up and down the stairs was when Cal's mom and I were married. Everything in the house seemed to be unchanged except that on this trip down it felt like someone doubled the number of stairs in the staircase.

At the bottom of the stairs I turned the corner to the left, walked through the screen door into the garage then down the driveway which was the longest walk I ever took in my life. That last jaunt to the hearse was surreal and like a slow motion movie that kept going on and on and on with no end in sight. Every step I took seemed to make the driveway grow two steps in length. His body was heavier than ever and I could see the hearse but deep inside I never wanted to make it to the hearse as I knew placing him inside was my last real goodbye... forever.

When I finally arrived at the hearse, I placed him on the stretcher in back. As they pushed the slider it was on back into the hearse I stood there in complete disbelief that this just actually happened. I felt like taking him back out in hopes that maybe he really wasn't dead. Maybe we could bring him back, cure his cancer and put this all behind us.

Maybe, maybe, maybe never came true and I stood there saying to myself that there was never anything anyone could do to me that would ever hurt this much. No one could ever mess up my life more than it was just messed up. I was never going to be afraid of anything or anyone ever again. This was the new reality for me and changed how I approach everything and everyone in life.

It would later transfer into what we do with Cal's Angels. For those who want the help and are open to beating the bully called cancer, I have vowed for it to be my life's mission to help them take the same path I have. Approach life with excited anticipation knowing that the worst thing that could ever happen to you has already happened so give it your all and succeed in all you do. Worst case scenario is you fail and so what? Any failure in the course of life pales in comparison to losing your child.

This is exactly what was going through our heads when Stacey and I started Cal's Angels a little over six months after Cal passed. We had no idea what we were doing or what we even wanted to raise money for but we knew we wanted to do something. We sent an email to our friends, neighbors and family asking them to join us in our dreams albeit we did not even know exactly what those dreams were. One week later in March of 2007, almost 30 people showed up in our living room one evening to help us create a dream — a dream that continues to evolve, change and become more exciting to be a part of every day.

Because of Cal's love of baseball, we first intended to provide scholarships to baseball players from the two high schools his teammates attend. It would be $10,000 to each winner payable over four years with no guarantee of continuing for four years unless certain criteria were met.

The name of the organization seemed to be pre-planned for us. Obviously Cal's for his name, All-Star because he was always on the all-star team and Angel because the last team he played on was the Angels coming up with Cal's All-Star Angel Foundation. Eerie to think this but the stars seem to have been aligning for it to play out this way before he was even diagnosed with leukemia.

In just over three months we held our first big event — the 1st Annual Dinner, Auction and Golf Outing on Friday, June 29th 2007. There were over 200 attendees and we raised over $73,000 after all expenses. With results like this at our very first event we knew we were on to something and could do a lot more than just scholarships.

In addition to the scholarships, we quickly decided to become a wish granter for children who were battling leukemia, providing financial assistance to their families for items like medical bills, car payments, food, parking passes and mortgage payments. Keeping with Cal's love for baseball, we also decided to financially assist the local little league baseball and softball programs, help the less fortunate families cover the cost of playing ball and provide funding to purchase equipment. Of course to be considered a viable charity and allow our supporters to legally deduct their donations, we had to become an IRS certified 501c3 charity.

One of our friends was a partner in a local law firm that had a team specializing in assisting charities with obtaining their 501c3 status. On a pro bono basis, they started the paperwork rolling by getting us incorporated but before any other work was done, our friend decided to leave the firm to start his own. As fate would have it neither him nor his new partner knew non-profit law so I was left to deal with his old firm who had subsequently decided they no longer wanted to help us. My files were given back and the only excuse was that it would "be a conflict of interest" if they assisted me. I even offered to pay but they still said no — seemed strange to me that it was a conflict of interest but okay, guess I'll start dialing to find a new attorney.

By the time attorney number eight told me they cannot assist with the front end in getting approval but would be happy to help with anything after that, I decided to give it a shot in getting the approval on my own. It's not the back end I was worrying about without there even being a front end. I went right to Google and started researching what others have done to get the coveted "501c3 Approval Letter" from the IRS along with reviewing the bylaws of other nonprofits both large and small.

Within five hours I had the plan all figured out and set my mind to working on it for at least two hours every day for a minimum of five days per week. After roughly 40 hours of time spent on the project I was done. There it was, right there in front of my eyes, the final application, the almost 70+ page key to creating the conduit that would connect the world's greatest donors to the most deserving recipients who are struggling with one of the worst nightmares known to man.

I issued a check to the IRS for their application and processing fees then sent the package off via certified mail which started the waiting game.

I was told by someone who has access to IRS information that our application finally hit the desk of an IRS clerk on a Friday and was approved ten calendar days later. Apparently, the swiftness of the approval, let alone on the first attempt, is unheard of in the nonprofit world. I believe it's just further proof of there being a master plan in place that this was all supposed to play out this way and continues to prove itself over and over by the staggering results we've experienced from day one.

From that very first fundraiser in June of 2007 where we raised over $73,000 after expenses, we have never looked back. Everything we have done has defied the odds and, despite starting right at the outset of the economic crisis that began in 2006-07 (or some say 2008), revenues have steadily increased year over year to where we sit in the fall of 2014 at $2 million with $3 million as the next goal.

There were the doubters and naysayers who asked how we were going to make a difference in a sea of thousands of non-profits in the Chicagoland area. Even Stacey and I doubted ourselves from time to time but along the way we learned a lot. Sometimes because we knew a little through past experiences and sometimes because we didn't know any better. We just did it and learned as we went along with the best things being learned through mistakes we had made.

We created an exciting organization rich with experiences not just for the recipients but for our donors, board members, employees and volunteers. Through these experiences lies the secret to keeping everyone interested and excited to come back and give of themselves to help us help others.

We created a young, new, vibrant, ever changing and evolving brand that resonates well with young and old alike. Never sitting still, never getting stagnant and listening to what others have to say, do or want are the keys to keeping it exciting and keeping it real.

We created a transparent platform where everybody knows everything we do with the money we raise. We run a tight ship out of our house and pay many of the bills that would otherwise go into running an organization out of our own pockets.

Up until recently, our accounting was a threefold process with checks and balances. First, by me making sure all the bills are paid. Second, by an outside accountant who does the reconciling but has no authority to make payments or withdrawals. The third and final step is performed by a CPA who does the cross checking, creating the financial statements and filing of all tax returns.

In keeping with transparency and separating ourselves from the financial side of things, we still have a threefold process but rather than me handling the front end, we have added a bookkeeper who is an individual unrelated to us and our family. She pays the bills and reconciles all accounts then directly reports the results to the outside accountant without Stacey or me having any involvement. Full, formal auditing is now standard practice.

We created a work environment where every employee, volunteer and board member is treated like family and, most importantly, we have fun while maintaining the highest levels of integrity, professionalism and ethics.

For the first six years I said I didn't want Cal's Angels to ever "become a business," but when I had to purchase a workers' compensation policy, I knew it had become a business. In the process of becoming a business, we became disruptors within the nonprofit world. I will stack Cal's Angels up against any of the big national non-profits and regular for profit corporations and beat most of them in every applicable business category.

Many will tell you that success is how you feel about what you've accomplished. Are you merely happy with where you are or are you truly satisfied with what you've accomplished? I'm happy but not satisfied as the Cal's Angels story has just begun.

I also like to take it further and say that if you're not pissing off a few folks — especially your competitors — you're certainly not doing something right. Not that you're doing anything wrong, you're just doing something they can't duplicate for whatever reason and it sticks in their craw. You're taking their market share or their fundraising dollars. You diminish their sense of self-worth and "disrupt their normal." Some will lash out at you in an attempt to bring you down and others will reach out with an olive leaf. For instance, we just had a huge humbling experience when one of the biggest nonprofit organizations in the world contacted us to "collaborate" and pick our brains on how we're able to "do what we do." It's at times like this that you know you're on the right path.

Furthering this notion and bolstering our pride is when someone who is involved with a lot of different charities and does a lot of studying on how businesses succeed and how businesses fail says that "Cal's Angels success is the wet dream of all charities." It's a quirky kind of funny and makes me think of that song "I Made It" by Kevin Rudolf, Birdman, Jay Sean and Lil' Wayne. While the song is about making it big for yourself, I twist it to be making it big for others to enjoy what you've accomplished especially these kids we help who are fighting cancer — they are the true heroes and I will continue to "make it" for them every day.

From my experiences and what I have learned about creating something from nothing through Cal's Angels, I now feel that I am ready to transfer what I've learned in the nonprofit world to the for profit world. I am looking for the right partners to join me in becoming a disruptor within the insurance industry by being different than the others starting with the simple notion of thinking about others first. Yes, as a business owner you may give something up in the short run but when you end up with a good majority of the best and brightest in the industry on your team, you all will succeed in the long run. Those who doubted you will get agitated, jealous and make excuses for their own failures while they really only need to chalk it up to either their own personal greed in looking out for number one once too often or just plain ol' resistance to the change that is required to succeed.

It can be done and I am determined to get it done because as I see it, the only real difference between a nonprofit organization and a for profit business is that one is governed by section 501c3 in the IRS code. The rest will be history and one day my team and I will each be singing, "I used to dream about the life I'm living now, I know that there's no doubt, I made it, I made it."

Don't get me wrong though. I am never going to give up the Cal's Angels gig — the job that pays the heart. It will be rewarding to be able to successfully run these two businesses simultaneously but yet autonomously so that no one ever feels like I'm using one to better the other. You can do good in both worlds and that is what I intend to do for the rest of my life — do good for others before doing good for myself. Nothing in this world gives me a deeper sense of self pride than this and nothing makes me feel more fulfilled than to see the results of what I've done for others.

CHAPTER ONE

My Cal: Part 1

*"Take care of all your memories.
For you cannot relive them."*

Bob Dylan, American Musician,
Singer-Songwriter, Artist and Writer

I can remember getting the call at work on June 6, 1993. The water of the soon to be mother of my first child broke and I needed to pick her up right away. I raced from the Woodfield area in Schaumburg, Illinois to O'Hare Airport, picked her up and made it to Palos Community Hospital in Palos Heights, Illinois in record time. I was speeding, swerving around cars and driving crazy going on the notion that no cop will hold it against me with a wife in labor. I made it free and clear, dropped her at the front door then met her inside.

I still remember the whole thing like it was yesterday — this was my first child, I was going to be a dad and I was filled with anticipation!

She was in labor forever with no progress in dilation so they decided to induce her to speed it up, but it still seemed like forever. Day turned into night and while we hung out in the room talking about what it's going to be like to be parents, it was storming like crazy outside. Widespread flooding, power outages and people stranded everywhere including those who were trying to come see us. I can remember this crazy movie on the TV at 1:00 a.m. with these huge rats invading some town and eating people. What a great birthing moment memory!

We were up all night and then the pace quickened as she started dilating accompanied by stronger and stronger contractions. Before I knew it, he was here and on June 7, 1993 my life changed forever, but never in my wildest dreams would I have guessed the path it would follow.

We kicked around a lot of names but I was torn a bit. I had always wanted to name my kids after sports stars but at the same time keep with the tradition of naming at least my first born son after me. I was surprised when I didn't get a fight from his mom when I compromised with myself and satisfied both desires by settling on a favorite. I did have a very valid reason, based on scientific evidence, for the choice I made.

For the first name, I thought back to when I played high school baseball. There was this young baseball player who was starting to make a name for himself and his name always stuck in my mind as being a cool name. I also looked into other sports stars who were great and those that were average. More often than not, the great ones had cool names while the rest generally carried an average name like Tom or Bob or Joe. I figured there must be some correlation between the level of coolness to the name and the level of performance one exhibits in his chosen sport. Using this expert analysis I decided to name him Cal after Cal Ripken. Not Calvin, Calhoun or anything else like that, just Cal, and Thomas for his middle name after me. Cal Thomas Sutter — with a name like that he was going to be a superstar.

From the very beginning Cal was a very cute baby. He never went through that awkward, adjusting to reality phase. I'm not saying this because he was my child, many people told me this including my father and when he says something like that, you know it's true because he was never one to say anything just to say it.

For as cute as Cal was, he knew how to test your patience. His mom doesn't really remember any of this and maybe it's the difference between moms and dads, but he had one of the worst cases of colic I have ever heard of or witnessed. On a daily basis he started crying around 3:00 or 4:00 p.m. and then the crying escalated into a terrifying noise—half scream at the top of your lungs and half cry with full on tears. This lasted until he eventually passed out between 8:00 and 10:00 p.m. He was barely able to take a bottle as the crying sometimes seemed like there was pain involved. It was unbelievable and it was at that point I realized why some people, without the ability to reason, snap in situations like this and wind up hurting or killing their child. It grates on your inner soul, deep into the skull and rattles your nerves. You have to remain focused on everything else going on while tuning the kid out enough to know what's going on with him but yet maintain sanity.

It was very hard to do but after a couple weeks I mastered it. I can remember Mark, my best friend from second grade on and Cal's Godfather, walking into our house during one of the peak scream/cry times. I was sitting in the rocker in the living room, Cal cradled in my arms wailing away, the TV up as loud as it could go so I could still hear it while rocking back and forth, staring straight ahead like I was in a trance. I didn't even know he came in until I saw him out of the corner of my eye staring at me and laughing. When I turned the TV down he said it was the freakiest scene he had ever seen — I looked like one of those crazy people who lost their minds, sitting and staring blindly at a wall for days on end. Everyone really felt bad for us, but no one wanted to take him, even for a night. I can honestly say that if he wasn't mine I would have never taken him, but he was mine and we were going to get through this, and we did.

Cal started to grow up and display an ultra-sensitive side to him. He was always concerned about other people's feelings even at a young age. He was also very funny and loved to make people laugh. He would dance wildly to songs and pretend to play instruments. One song he totally loved was Baby Likes to Rock It by the Tractors. He would pretend like he was jamming on the piano, run around like a crazy man and dance wildly, holding onto the spindles on the staircase. We would laugh every time because it was truly that funny.

I remember so many other things Cal did or said that were just down right funny; I mean belly aching from laughing so hard funny.

When he was potty training we had this little plastic toilet that was low to the floor so he could get on and off easily. He wouldn't stay in the bathroom by himself so we brought it into the kitchen where he sat for hours while we kept feeding him juice so he would pee. Three full bottles later and no pee, his mom gave up and went to work. I was determined to get him to go but in the interim, I myself had to go so I snuck out to go to the bathroom.

When I came back he was gone and the back sliding door was open. What the … where did he go? I ran to the back door and out onto the deck calling his name. No answer, so I started down the steps at a more frantic pace and called his name again. As I came around the back side of the deck he came running from behind the tree line separating our backyard from our neighbors. He went up the steps and into the house wearing nothing but a little tee shirt that stopped at his waist.

Curious, I went around the tree line and scanned the area. Up on the neighbor's patio was a pile of fresh poop. How do I know it was fresh? It was cool out and the steam was slowly rising into the air. And it was a big one. Looked like a large dog dropped a load, so I decided that's what they would think and I left it as I darted back into the house.

"Wow!" is all I could think to myself about this situation and when I tried asking Cal why he didn't do that in the toilet all he could do was give a blank stare like I had two heads.

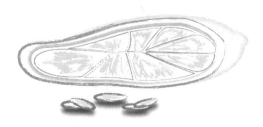

CHAPTER TWO

Let's Paint This Picture and Set the Stage

"Who you are today is a compilation of everything you have experienced in life no matter what age you were when it was experienced ..."

Tom Sutter

Yes, I know it's unusual to use your own quote to begin a chapter in your own book but you will learn throughout my story that I really don't follow the "status quo" set of parameters in most aspects of my life. Besides that, you will also quickly learn that I do have a lot to say on most topics probably because of the way my life has played out from the very beginning through a series of events that molded me into the experience rich person I am today.

The single most significant event in my life was my oldest child Cal becoming ill and ultimately passing away. He was diagnosed with leukemia in June of 2005, fought a gruesome, drawn out battle for 14 ½ months and eventually succumbed to the cancer that ravaged his way-too-young body on August 28, 2006. While some may look it at as a series of events leading to a single outcome, I consider all of this to be one single event.

How I handled it then and continue to handle it even to this day has a lot to do with the other events of my life that shaped me into who I am today.

So let's start at the beginning and see how all of this fits together. Some of you will see yourself in parts of this, or even all of it, while others are associated with those who have had similar experiences in life and yes, I know, some will be completely shocked by what they are about to read, finding some of it hard to believe.

Each of us lives in a world of possibilities that doesn't need to be restricted or hindered by how we grew up and what we have experienced in life. With everything that has happened to each of you, you can either feel sorry for yourself or treat what has happened as a gift. Everything that occurs in your life either creates an opportunity for growth or an obstacle to prevent you from growing — you get to choose.

The good news is that, yes, you can get through it all, survive and use it to thrive in all you do. If you can take this message and apply it to your life in whatever way is best for you, my story will have succeeded. My number one goal is to help you learn not to dwell on the past and let the negatives of the past shape your future, but look forward to creating a whole new path in life for yourself and those around you.

Childhood and the Negatives of Chaos

From all accounts of those who knew her best, my mother was an extreme overachiever in her younger years. According to what I was told, she skipped two grades along the way, graduated high school at sixteen and went into the workforce in data processing when the field was just being developed.

Back then in my younger days she was a good-looking young lady that drew the attention of men. She was of medium build, solid, not fat, and could pack a wallop in her punch. Her father was a street smart street fighter who I believe taught her a few things on inflicting pain — she knew how to fight. A telltale sign of knowing when someone knows how to fight is when they get into the set position, staggered step, both closed fists up by their shoulders or a little higher to protect the face and the thumbs are out.

My mom grew up an only child in a three-bedroom brick split-level home in Hillside, Illinois, that was built right after World War II. I recall it being a decent neighborhood, an older neighborhood, with big trees in every yard. My grandparents had a couple of rather large apple trees in the backyard and a maple tree that we used to climb as kids.

Her dad, my grandfather, was a man's man. Despite his tall and thin frame, he looked, acted and talked tough. He was a World War II veteran and earned his living as a truck driver. He would spend his winters out in Lake Havasu, Arizona, where the actual original London Bridge was relocated from London.

I remember spending a lot of time with him — some of my best life lessons came from his wisdom. Like I said, he was street smart and he knew his way around and how to make it in life. My all-time favorite quote came from the grandfather who refused to be called anything but "Pop" (pronounced 'pup') because, as he always said, old people are called by other names such as grandpa, grandfather, granddad, etc.

Pop told me, "Tommy, don't ever tell a lie because lies are way too hard to remember. Always tell the truth because it's something you can't forget even if you try."

There were other great quotes and an infinite amount of wisdom that came from his vast array of life experiences. He told me to love everyone until they prove you shouldn't, and to never take crap from anyone, unless the consequences of not taking the crap are too dire. This is a lesson I should have followed much earlier in life.

As you can probably tell, he was a wise man, everyone loved Pop — even my buddies loved him. Who else's grandfather would someone's 20-something-year-old friends want to go to a bar with and hang out? Going to his hangouts was like something out of the show Cheers when Norm walked in — everyone would get excited and shout out, "Koby," which was his nickname, short for his elongated polish last name of Kobylinski.

Who also could say their dad bailed their grandfather out of jail for fighting when he was in his 70's? Pop decked a guy half his age and knocked him out cold. Talk about crazy!

Another defining story is when he had Tuberculosis and the doctor also discovered he had had a heart attack at some point in the past, but Pop didn't know it. I was there when the doc asked him about it and he said he was clueless, then looked at me and said half laughing like he was explaining something funny, yet cool, "Hey Tommy, maybe it was that time I passed out and fell off the bar stool. I thought I was hammered but maybe that's when I had the heart attack!"

The doc looked at me and asked if he drank a lot and I covered for him by saying, "Heck no; he just ties one on once in a while." I don't think the doc bought it.

Pop called himself the 'Polish lover' and the 'crazy Pollock'. No matter what you called him, he was a good man with a big heart who would do anything for just about anyone, especially if you were a friend, and he had a heck of a lot of friends.

The exact information needed to piece the beginnings of my parents' relationship together was never really shared and the details are fuzzy at best, but I'm giving it a try based on piecing together broken stories I overheard. My mom and dad worked at Keebler after high school back in the mid-1960's. Though they did not know each prior to working there, I'm of the understanding it didn't take long for them to meet as they both were working with computer punch cards — a job usually performed by the men while the stereotypical position for the women was secretarial in nature.

They married shortly thereafter and I was born when she was 19 and my dad was 21 — roughly seven months after they married, which means I was either a preemie or I am the reason why they don't provide many details. I honestly believe many of her actions and inactions were shaped by her having to come out of the workforce before she really wanted to or was ready to do so. She instantly went from a promising career woman with an "I want to work and show these boys how it's done" attitude to a stay-at-home mom.

Before getting into the interrelationships of the family I want to paint you a picture of my surroundings throughout my childhood.

My parents' first home was an apartment in Melrose Park, Illinois, and I was born down the street at Gottlieb Memorial Hospital. My mom tells the stories of traversing the streets during the blizzard of '67 while pregnant with me — drifts up to her belly, cars stranded everywhere and no means of communication like we have nowadays with cell service and all.

We eventually moved to a ranch-style house with a big back yard and several big trees in a middle class neighborhood in Elk Grove Village, Illinois. The appliances were all drab olive green with wood paneling on the walls. The neighborhood was mostly ranch houses and all pretty much the same — strikes me as being one of those post-war Sears brand manufactured home neighborhoods you read about in the history of housing.

My brother was born in town at Alexian Brothers Hospital two-and-a-half years after me. I can remember watching TV shows on Saturday nights such as the Wonderful World of Disney, Sonny and Cher, and Captain and Tennille. We didn't stay long in that neighborhood as I can recall only attending Grantwood Elementary School through first grade, and then we moved on.

Before second grade started, they sold the ranch house with plans to move to a brand new house on the new side of town which was referred to as moving "west of 53." I can remember looking at the models — it was a large dogwood-style split-level house and my parents were excited to start new with a bigger and better place.

But there were some labor strikes and it took two years to build, so we lived in a townhouse in Hanover Park, Illinois, with my mother driving us 15 miles or so to school each way, each and every day. I can remember the community pool and the adult pool at the complex with the fenced walls you couldn't see through. Rumors carry some crazy stories about that place.

A few years after moving in to the new house, my parents splurged on a built-in swimming pool with a slide in the back yard. We instantly became the popular kids others wanted as friends. We also had a large 15x15 garden where we grew our own vegetables. I learned a lot from that experience — when things are fresh and when they are not and how to pick them for the best results possible, which is probably why I'm so fussy when picking out produce at the grocery store.

We also always had dogs — mostly black labs and eventually a white German Shepherd to make it interesting. We also intermittently had hamsters, birds and fish, making it feel like a mini zoo around the house.

For the longest time my brother and I each had our own bedrooms. Then when I was 16 my parents started building family number two. With an "oops" as the beginning phase and the planned playmate for my sister (the oops) when I was 19. They converted the back playroom in the basement to a bedroom for me until I went off to college.

My brother was moved down there after my second sister was born, which worked out fine since I was away at college — we only crossed paths when I was home, which became a rare occurrence when he went away to college. It was odd when we were both home as there was only one bed to share — a king size water bed that we were told to like it or move out on our own, adding the often used phrase by my father, "If you want to start paying the bills then you can start making the rules."

Guess it's something you just learn to live with.

The year I graduated from college, they moved from Elk Grove Village to a large house with an almost acre lot in Sleepy Hollow, Illinois. It was not a childhood home of mine insofar as the memories go, but when I was going through my divorce, I moved in there with them and they allowed me to sleep in a twin bed in an upstairs bedroom, but I had to keep everything I owned, including my clothes, in the basement.

My mother is an extreme hoarder and had every closet in the house filled after completely over stuffing her own huge walk-in closet. Though I had room for my clothes down there, the basement was also stuffed to the gills with enough food for my parents and two sisters to live for a year — granted most would spoil, but you get the point. There was so much that she had no idea what was there.

I remember finding a jar of maraschino cherries tucked away behind everything in the back of the fridge with a Phar Mor price tag on it. No biggie except Phar Mor had gone out of business five or six years earlier —

she had no idea it was even there nor did she know she had nine bricks of Philadelphia Cream Cheese tucked away in the fridge — most six months or more past expiration.

I remember my dad once saying not to get rid of the spoiled food or tell my mom it was there because all she'll do is throw it out and buy more to keep their two refrigerator freezer units full. Plus, the freezer-only unit had to be duck taped shut to keep all the food from popping the door open.

From my perspective, the relationship I had with my mom was always one of the love-hate varieties. When I think about my early years, life was chaotic at best. I believe a lot of my mom's attitude was directed specifically at me, but over the years I have come to know there was a reason for it, albeit not an acceptable reason, but a reason nonetheless.

I was the first to be born and based on "off the cuff" comments she made I honestly believe I represented to her the reason her career was ruined — her life dreams flushed down the toilet.

Being an informal, self-taught student of psychology and self-study on what drives certain behaviors, my mom is a classic example of why someone turns to mood altering substances. I'm not talking drugs, but to sum up my mom, her fondness for alcohol, actually just plain old beer to be exact, and it was Schlitz for the longest time, brought out the mean side of her, which manifested itself in frequent bouts of anger, both verbal and physical.

On more than one occasion her "fondness" left me with some pretty serious physical wounds, but more than the physical abuse, the emotional abuse from the belittling, shaming, ridiculing and threats, plus terrorizing by making sure I feared her occurred on a regular basis.

From what I can remember, if I wanted to catch her when she wasn't drinking a beer, I had to get her in the morning after she woke up around 9:00 or 10:00 a.m. until sometime in the early afternoon. By dinner time, it was usually too late; she was on her way to putting down her usual 12-pack a night; sometimes more, sometimes less. And the more she put down, the more violent she got when she was angered and the more verbally abusive she became.

She made me feel like a piece of crap and teased me because I was a dork, overweight, had buck teeth, looked silly, had some quirks, and hated the smell of cigarette smoke — I remember one time waking up with my parents' full ash tray in my cereal bowl to "teach me a lesson" and learn to deal with it. But why should I be that upset? At least they were nice about it as they even laid out a spoon for me.

What is still interesting even to this day is how it would either take a lot or just a little by hitting one of the few "hot buttons" to get her to fly off the handle in an instant. And when she did, it was complete out of control behavior, made worse with the alcohol acting like fuel on the fire. At her worst, she would beat my brother and me with a belt or a wooden spoon. I'm not talking about just getting hit once, but repeated beating until we had welts and even bled on a few occasions.

I remember her even beating on my dad as he would just take it without fighting back. She would throw things at him, call him some of the worst names I have ever heard anyone call another human being, let alone their spouse, hit him with her hands, pots, pans and anything she could get her hands on.

One of the times she was the most charged up was because my dad suggested she was being too harsh on me (one of the "hot buttons") resulting in game over — she set out to show him what too harsh really was. I remember it exactly because it was one of those "shocks to the system" you can't forget.

The screaming, the name calling, the hitting, the throwing of objects, the breaking of objects, then my dad leaving for weeks, something that occurred several times — chaotic moments that I was never able to shake.

When my dad was gone my mom would come home with boyfriends or we'd go on vacation with some guy. I had no idea who this guy was, but we did go, all the while acting like a family. Then my dad was back — then the fights would start again and then he'd leave again. You almost have to create a flow chart to follow these things.

One vivid childhood memory I have is at a party at my aunt's house. With my mom being an only child all of the aunts and uncles are on my dad's side. They were all getting loaded when all of a sudden you could hear screaming in the kitchen.

It was more like blood curdling screeching with my mom calling my aunt an f'in bitch and every other name in the book. I ran in behind the adults only to see my mom holding my aunt down towards the ground by the shirt collar with her left hand and pounding her face with the other, closed fisted-style and thumb out. My dad and uncles were trying to stop it and my mom was flailing wildly at everyone, screaming vulgarities at all of them.

Amidst the chaos they eventually got her off my aunt only to find my mom now grabbing bottles and cups and hitting the guys every chance she got. A couple of the bottles broke and there was a lot of swearing, yelling and crazy "stuff" happening. Looking back, it was like a scene out of a horror flick where the monster is attacking the village and is eventually subdued by the villagers. They literally had to carry her out and throw her in the car.

We sped off with her still going on about my aunt and how dare she say that and how dare my dad allow his sister to talk like that to his wife, how he's a wimp for not standing up to everyone. It was crazy stuff to listen to but then it got even crazier with her getting out at the red light under the premise that she's going back "to finish the bitch off" because, apparently, no one was going to talk to my mom like that even though she was never really clear what was said.

Felt bad for my dad though — he left the car running with an eight- and six-year-old in it while he chased his drunk wife down the road to get her back in the car. Seemed like forever while sitting through several cycles of the stoplight, cars honking then going around us, but they eventually came back. Then on the way driving home, the alcohol hit her good and she puked out the window with some of it coming back in on me. Not sure if she ate oatmeal, but it looked like it, sticking to my blue, furry, crushed velvet, shag carpet-like coat with the built in tie-down hood.

Why do I tell you all this in such great detail? I want you to understand that I do have a very vivid memory of situations that are what I call "shocks to the system." Any of this is in that category while some of the more trivial, mundane things are not in that category, such as people's names and even sometimes faces, I have a hard time with those but not situations like this.

Anyway, back to the family.

My dad was a total enabler. He started working later and later, even picking up a second job "to pay the bills," but I really think it was to avoid being around my mom, all the while leaving us at the house with this woman who tended to get out of control. It was an, "I love you … no, I hate you but wait, I do love you" situation.

You never knew when you were going to be loved or hated — classic results of alcohol-fueled situations. It was rough on school days, not knowing what the environment would be like when you opened the door.

My dad allowed the bullying from my mom. He wouldn't stick up for either of us. When I was about 15 or 16 I asked him why he didn't stand up for his kids against mom. I felt back then, and definitely know now, that when physical and mental abuse is dished out like that on a regular basis, proper emotional, psychological and social development is nearly impossible.

Rather than provide any answer or explanation, he told me not to blame anyone for my problems and sort of looked at me like I'm the one with the issues. I told him that I wasn't blaming, just pointing out the facts. He shrugged it off like it was no big deal.

But it was a big deal; I was growing up to be a lot like my mother and I didn't, and still don't, want to be like that, but I know I will always feel a natural tendency to act in certain ways when presented with certain situations.

By saying I don't want to grow up acting or reacting like her, a conversation my brother and I had a few years back comes to mind. It was regarding the topic of questions and how someone said there's no such thing as a stupid question.

Without skipping a beat, he said that's wrong and that he knows of one really stupid question, which was asked on several occasions. After we had pushed my mom to the breaking point and she lashed out in anger, leaving us banged up and bawling, she would tell us, "Stop crying; do you want me to give you something to really cry about?"

Though we laugh now, it really isn't funny because it was obvious she already gave us something to cry about, so why on God's earth would we want something to really cry about? This hurts plenty!

There was a run-in with my mom around this time. I was maybe 15 and she went to crack me one across the face for some unknown reason, but there was no way I was letting it happen.

All the horrible things came flashing back all at once, like breaking models I took months to build, or smashing trophies I won in sports across the desk all because there was a speck of dust on it after I dusted, then beating me because I caused her to chip the desk with the model or trophy, calling me names, smacking me, ripping up clothes I bought with my own money because I didn't clean to her unrealistic specs. And on and on and on — it all hit me at once. I caught her hand in my open hand and closed down on it using it as a lever to push her to the ground telling her that never again was she going to hit me.

One part I feel bad about is that this happened when she had a cast on her foot — I think it was a broken ankle, but she was just about healed. Didn't stop her from playing martyr and how she was being abused as an invalid. I told her to grow up, stop playing the games and to leave me alone — I did it all in the same crazy voice, using the same antics she used to taunt me, bully me and abuse me.

The bully had been bullied and little did I know, this was foreshadowing what was to come in my life.

A couple years later, my dad and I had another run-in on the same subject. This time I remember getting really pissed at my dad and yelling at him for never sticking up for us and never protecting my brother or me from Mom.

I'll never forget the horrible look he gave me while he told me in order to keep the peace he would never interfere with my mother's rules. It was at that point I really acted like my mom and pushed my dad onto the bed in their bedroom. I called him horrible names, telling him to get up and fight like a man. I was so angry at him and I was ready to do to him what he allowed Mom to do to us, but he wouldn't fight back, only telling me to leave in such a calm voice it was frightening.

I packed up and went back to college, as I did not want to go to bed there only to never awaken again.

Our relationship was never good in the first place, but after that, our relationship was never the same again. For the longest time I thought he was a great dad as he always coached my baseball teams but, actually, that was all he really did with us. He never talked with us, learn about us, our lives, our friends or anything — he was an MIA dad who found time to coach baseball for a couple months per year and for maybe 20 games at most.

He would shake hands with us, but never hug us or kiss us because that was "gay." I really don't remember one hug or kiss from my dad, nor do I remember one from his dad, my grandfather. I don't really remember much at all about my dad's side; we never spent much time with them and his parents were kind of cold and distant towards us anyway.

Now Pop was different — he hugged and kissed us on the cheek until the day he died when I was in my 30's. It wasn't embarrassing at all with Pop, but he was the only guy. Not even my brother could hug or kiss me. I now know you have to hug and kiss your kids. There's nothing wrong or strange about it. They're your kids.

And it's also completely okay to hug your brother, your relatives and guy friends. I learned that it actually feels pretty darn good — if you don't do it, try it. It may be awkward at first, but as long as neither of you lock your leg around behind the other guy's leg while hugging, it's not awkward and completely acceptable in all circles.

I also remember my dad being very cheap. His parents grew up during the Depression era. He was one of the cheapest guys you would ever want to meet. I remember him getting upset with my mom if she bought us anything.

At his request, or at least that's what my mom tells us, we would get a six-pack of white t-shirts, one for every day of the week but Sunday and we wore jeans with those. On Sundays, we got to wear something different — usually our plaid polyester pants and a nice shirt so that we could go out to "eat nice" at places like the Milk Pail in Elgin, Illinois.

I can only remember taking one bath per week, which was on Saturdays before watching the Saturday shows I mentioned. We ate pizza that was delivered from Jake's Pizza and Pub. The other nights we had a sink-full of water to wash up in unless we were so filthy my mother would be "forced" to give us another bath in the same week.

We would have to bring home our brown paper bag and plastic bags for school lunches in order to make them last the whole week. If we didn't abide by the "lunch bag" rule, we would not get another one, but it was "our choice" if that occurred. About fourth grade, we got lunch boxes — mine was "Sigmund and the Sea Monsters" themed.

Once I got to high school, I bought my own clothes if I wanted anything other than plain old jeans and t-shirts. I had parachute pants and all of the hip stuff because I worked since I was 12 as a caddy and cutting grass. Eventually I progressed into regular jobs as a teen.

As for the jeans when we were younger — they were Toughskins from Sears. The great thing about Toughskins was that if you were able to wear a hole in the knee you got a free pair, so my mom would make us keep wearing them even after they were too small until we got a hole in the knee. She would then go to exchange it for the larger size only to run in to the manager who would say the exchange had to be for the same size. That poor guy didn't realize you don't tell my mom something like that; she would be all over the manager's case and cause such a commotion in the store that they would always cave in just to shut her up and get her out of the store.

While he was too embarrassed to go with her, I know my dad was so proud of his woman during those moments, probably one of the reasons why he put up with the other crap. I think he only had to buy two pairs of Toughskins for me my entire life — one forest green and one burgundy — when I was five and never spent a dime again except for the white t-shirts and polyester duds for "eatin' nice" on Sundays. I might have had a third pair in junior high which was navy blue but I'm not 100% sure. What was really classy is that every once in a while we got the white t-shirts with the pockets until the kids at school called me a nerd. Then I begged them to just get the plain ones.

What was extremely fashionable was when my mom made us our Sunday duds for a year or two. I can remember one really hip short sleeve button down that felt like thicker rippled drapery material complete with flashy orange, red, yellow and a splash of white and blue design — it went great with the homemade reddish burgundy pants with the fumbling zipper that didn't work real well.

Do I have all bad memories? No. There were good memories too, especially when she was in her mode of trying to make up for being mean and nasty. Those were some great times because then we'd get anything we wanted and life was pretty darn good.

Christmas was always a time for making up — we were always loaded down with a lot of presents. But, in general, it was not knowing how to act or react because we weren't always mature enough to know if she was drinking, not drinking, hung-over or trying to make up for something. Sometimes I thought she was just baiting us into something before turning on us — it was a tug of war of emotions that caused confusion in the emotional maturation process.

As crazy as it was, I had to learn to cope and I now know I became what some deem to be a co-dependent. I was totally attached to my mom to the point it was way overboard and weird at best. She had that way of creating and fostering dependency.

Crazy, but it's a psychological situation you find over and over where the opposite result to the norm actually becomes the norm. I learned how to mitigate some of the chaos by sucking up to her and that habit carried over to people in general. I would say I was sorry for things that I was not really sorry for just to keep the peace.

I would escape by listening to loud heavy metal music that would draw me in and take me to another place. Heavy metal was augmented by adding rap — not easy rap, but gangsta' rap. What's funny to those that know me though, is that I also enjoy country, pop and hip-hop — to me, it's all good, but depends on my mood at the time.

Today I don't have much of a relationship with my parents, mostly by my own choice because I have come to learn that none of this represents the right way to run your life. Any professional would tell you that still having a relationship would prove I have not broken free of that environment and all that it brings.

My siblings are still sucked in to it with my sister going so far as to ostracizing me and asking if I think my mother is the devil or something.

While I don't think she's the devil, I will tell you she is the product of her environment growing up and she never broke the cycle. Pop told me on several occasions that his biggest regret in life is not taking my mom and leaving my grandma.

From what my mom says and Pop confirms, my grandma was as mean as they come, but quite the opposite to us, her grandkids — nice as pie and twice as sweet. It was hard to believe my mom's stories, but I could never doubt Pop's word on anything … ever.

It took me a while but I eventually chose to break the cycle of chaos and make it different for my kids and my family. I'm also happy to say that it turned out the same for my brother though he still has a relationship with our parents — not fully broken free, but he does not transfer the chaos into his family life from what I can tell.

Chapter Two Takeaways — Discussion Topics

- **Parents need to always be conscious that they are role models and their children are like sponges soaking up everything they say and do.**

- **An individual's natural reactionary tendencies to situations are subconsciously directed by what shaped their early years.**

- **The mental, emotional and physical environment you create for your children will determine their "normal."**

- **Hopefully this cycle is good; if not, it will continue until someone is strong enough to break it and say enough is enough.**

- **If a "new normal" ever needs to be created, it is not an easy process and can be a work-in-progress that can take a lifetime.**

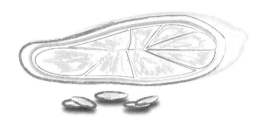

CHAPTER THREE
What's a Chreaster?

"Do not judge or you too will be judged.
For in the same way you judge others,
you will be judged, and with the measure you use,
it will be measured to you."

Matthew 7:1-2

Both my mother and father were raised Catholic. On the surface we appeared to be a very strict Catholic family — Church, CCD, Communion, Confirmation and no meat on Fridays during Lent.

I say "on the surface" because it was all for show or out of habit. The reality is we, as a family, did not follow everything in the faith except going to church and the usual, expected rituals of CCD, etc. We were never taught the meaning behind faith, God and a higher power, so we really didn't know what it was all about, except that, "You better not sin or you're going to hell where your inner soul will burn for eternity."

I also remember my mom telling me that in hell there would be rabid pigs chewing little pieces of my toes off as they slowly work their way up my leg over the course of hundreds of years all because my brother and I fought. Scared the crap out of me for sure and really not something that made me want to believe but rather made me feel like I had to believe.

I'm sure that, because of the way it was presented to us, my brother and I felt as if we were being forced to attend church with my father in our younger years rather than being excited or even willing to go. I really don't remember my mother attending with us, not even at holiday time, except when she had to put on a show like at a Communion, Baptism, Confirmation, etc.

We got older and my father waned in his commitment to the Church. I remember several occasions where my brother and I were dropped off at the foot of the large, looming concrete steps in front of the church and then picked up when Mass ended. I'm guessing this made them feel better about saying we attended church like a good Catholic family does.

Now, while I said that I grew up going to church, it actually changed sometime around junior high or high school. That is when we became those holiday churchgoers more commonly known as the Chreaster family, Christmas and Easter. At the time that was completely fine with me. But what was very confusing is why my mother could not even get up for two simple days of church per year while spouting how we needed to have God in our lives to save us from the Devil. I didn't know the reason for her absence back then, but it resulted in me having no qualms about pushing back against religion in general. As soon as I was able to stand up to the "inconvenience" of religion, I stopped going to church.

What bolstered my rebellion against religion is that the scientific method was taught in school, making it that much more difficult to believe in a higher power. However, as time went on, I got to the point where so many things were happening and I realized how each little part of any of the sequences played off the other parts of the sequence that formed a complete outcome that made sense. When this happens over and over you just know there has to be a reason for all of it to have played out like it did — none of it just happened by coincidence or by chance but rather appears to be part of a master plan.

Because of my awareness to all of these "things" playing out, I now know that I never stopped believing; I just stopped practicing my faith. As a way to justify this, I would catch myself saying there is no God, but, deep down, I always knew there was. It's just that the way my faith had been almost jokingly drilled into me, it left a negative connotation on the whole concept of God and faith. Moreover, being a teen, it was interfering with everything in my life that was fun and about being a teen with wants, needs and desires for nothing other than having a good time.

As we're traveling down this road of church, faith, belief, God and religion, I want to make sure it's clear that I do not now nor have I ever proclaimed to be an extremely religious or even righteous individual, nor even what some would call a "Holy Bible Thumper" saying, "You're going to go to Hell if you do not go to church," but that doesn't mean I haven't always believed to one degree or another.

That distancing from attending church and living a Christian lifestyle rippled through to my first marriage which was formalized at the courthouse.

My first wife was Lutheran, but not a regular church-goer. We really only went to church on a handful of holidays plus the usual Baptism, Communion, Confirmation, etc. in the eight years we were together — the typical Chreaster churchgoing lifestyle I was used to in my teens and beyond. I'm not sure of her excuse, but I was still in "church avoidance."

She was right there with me; thus the result was a non-Christian home and lifestyle for our three children. The main reason for any church activity was to get our kids baptized and those occasional holiday visits.

Shortly after my divorce I met my wife of today, Stacey, and started going to church again. She was attending a Lutheran church and I joined her. Second time around I married the girl my heart and soul were waiting for and it was in a church this time, the Lutheran Church.

Eventually, Stacey and I started going to a non-denominational Christian church, dividing our time between Christ Community Church in St. Charles, Illinois and Harvest Bible Chapel in Elgin, Illinois.

We have never gone every Sunday, but it became a bigger part of our lives.

My change in how I believe evolved from being a "forced believer" under what I consider to be false pretenses, into being a "hard to believe" believer and now a true believer.

My belief in God sure was tested when we went through this battle with Cal's leukemia. After Cal passed away, I was so mad, no, let's get it straight, pissed off at God that I went out to Cal's favorite ball field sometime after midnight one summer night, stood on the pitcher's mound where he last pitched and challenged Him to come down so I could give Him a fresh can of whoop ass equivalent to the hurt he dished out to me by taking my son, my oldest child, my 13-year-old boy who was so full of love, life and the thrill of it all.

It is really interesting to me to witness the different ways people come at believing. Some people have a thought process in terms of believing that they would rather error on the side of believing just in case there is something, because if you do not believe and there is a God, you just bought yourself some serious issues after the point of no return.

This one never made sense to me. Part of me says that if you only believe because you are afraid of what might happen if you do not believe, that is not being a true believer; that is just living a lie and He knows the difference.

Today, I can firmly say that I am a true believer because I do not think that anything in my life nor in this beautiful, complicated world of ours just happened by chance. I believe there is something out there; I call that God. It is too hard to explain things without believing there is a God.

It gives people hope that there is something beyond this life and that when they die it is not just over. It is way too hard to believe that all of this was created for us to enjoy only for the short time while we are here and then it's gone with nothing to experience afterwards. Cal was only here for thirteen years. Was our world created with the intention of him enjoying it for only thirteen years and then it's over? What about those who die even younger? Or those who live for 100 years — is that long enough to fully utilize and appreciate all of this?

I do not think so. I also believe it is the hope that we will be reunited with those we love. There is hope for more than what we have here right now. It is almost ironic that I met a girl who goes to church and even more so that she is the daughter of June and Ward Cleaver. Her upbringing was a complete contrast to the rebel rouser I was for pretty much all my years after seventh grade ending somewhere around the time between when Cal was born and my daughter Jessica was born where I realized it was finally time to take life seriously.

When I met Stacey and started going to church again, that was not so much because I suddenly felt I needed to and should go. It was more like you meet a girl who goes to church and says, "Come to church with me." If you really like her and want to get somewhere with her, what do you do? Pretty simple answer to that question — you go to church with her. I know Stacey knew that inside I was hesitating, but I wanted to be with her enough that I went to church.

Before I knew it I was sitting there at Immanuel Lutheran Church in East Dundee, Illinois and Pastor Yonker was preaching. He is not just one of the best preachers I have ever heard but one of the best overall speakers I have ever heard. The first time I heard him, I thought his message only took about five minutes.

When I looked at my watch, though, it had been almost half an hour — completely captivating and to top it off he hugged everyone who would hug him when the service was over!

Now, we find the same thing at Christ Community Church and Harvest Bible Chapel. I do not even know an hour has passed, that is how good these services are and that is what we look for in a church and a service.

Growing up Catholic and this being a Lutheran church aroused my curiosity. Is it different? It was thought provoking and I was never concerned about different worship service styles. I just go with the flow as I do with most things in life.

I did wonder what was going to happen. It was not awkward, but I wondered if God was looking at me and saying, "Hey, you're only here because that girl you want to get together with is here, but that is not what this church is all about."

I asked myself a lot of questions like, "Am I getting myself into something that I really do not want to be involved in?"

"Should I just run and move on to the next young lady who catches my eye?"

"Or should I just tough it out and see what happens?"

I did "tough it out" and when I look back on it I think, "Thank God I did!"

It was a decision point in my life that could have dramatically changed everything. Instead I married that church-going girl at Immanuel Lutheran Church in January of 2005. We did it in early January so that we could keep the Christmas theme for our service and reception. I have to say it was pretty cool — I just love the Christmas season.

You should see our house — my nickname amongst friends and family is Clark Griswold from Christmas Vacation. Now, my son Ryan has the bug and we decorate together sometimes until two or three in the morning for several nights in a row just to get it done. It's not tacky like the Griswold's though, a lot of lights and done up very nicely.

I did not notice much of a difference between the Catholic and Lutheran services except that the Lutheran was a little more relaxed and the sermon was definitely more real and powerful. At Christ Community Church, or Harvest, or even Willow Creek Church in South Barrington, Illinois, it is even more relaxed and they have some pretty hip bands that play Christian rock and younger gen music. I think that if my experience in growing up had been in a church like any of these I probably would have wanted to attend and been an enthusiastic believer all along.

While Stacey, the kids and I are all believers, we do not go to church with any regularity and for some stretches of time we do not attend church at all. Not to make excuses, but we have six kids, five live with us full-time who are all active in sports, some are two sports at a time. When counting Cal's Angels, I have two full-time jobs and writing this book is a part-time gig. My wife has one full time job with Cal's plus however many more you want to add in with the kids.

Am I making an excuse?

On the one hand, yes.

But on the other hand, I am not.

I always make time to pray and thank God for all the things and people in my life. For my family, for my employer who took care of my family during Cal's illness, for my friends, for being able to run Cal's Angels and, especially, for having Stacey in my life.

I thank God for everything and yes, I know my son died but I could have lost everything at that point and I did not. As a result, I am thankful that I came through all of it so well and that it has a meaning beyond any one particular moment in time.

I know that God understands this, but I also know that there are believers who do not. Probably because of my upbringing, we do not expect our children to do any more or less than we do. If we go, they go. If we do not, they do not. We let them make up their own minds to go on their own when we don't go but when we do go, we go as a family. We make time for God as a family because for us God, faith and religion are family things.

The events in my life are all a cumulative effect adding up to where I am today. They all play off of one another; they are integral and sequential parts of each other that cannot be separated.

Chapter Three Takeaways — Discussion Topics

ATTITUDES:

- Your attitude towards religion and faith will shape your children's attitudes as well.

- Only "Bible Thumpers" should go to church.

- Believing because you're afraid not to is one of the signs of a true believer.

THE BIBLE:

- What does the Bible say about going to church? How about Jesus? Life after death? Heaven?

CHURCH:

- Do you have to go to church if you believe in God, pray and thank God for all you have on a daily basis?

- Can your faith be strong if you don't go to church?

- Are there any valid excuses to skip going to church?

GOD:

- Is it wrong to challenge God?

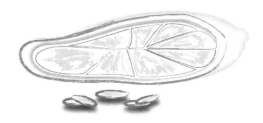

CHAPTER FOUR

Broken Bones Can Be Good for the Mind, Body and Spirit

"The quality of a person's life is in direct proportion to their commitment to excellence, regardless of their chosen field of endeavor."

Vince Lombardi, American Football Player,
Coach and Executive

Breaking my leg in seventh grade was one of those "shocks to the system" that made me who I am today, and was the second biggest event in my life.

It was a cool, faintly grey day in the early spring a couple months before school was out. The grass was just turning green but the leaves had not yet popped on the trees and bushes. I was with three of my friends and we all had the same great idea — two guys would be the riders on bikes and two others would tie ropes onto the back of the bikes and get pulled around the neighborhood on skateboards.

My skateboard was sky blue, the thicker plastic version, with chrome brackets that held on the dark red wheels. I'm sure I got that one not for the looks but because it was cheaper than the professional wooden ones. However, in this case, it didn't really matter how good the skateboard was. The rock it hit was big enough to stop the board in its tracks and the momentum I had going launched me through air. The way I had the rope wrapped around my wrist and forearm prevented me from letting go. My goal was to wrap it good enough so I wouldn't let go while cruising down the street — never thought I would hit something and need to let go.

I don't really remember anything after the initial "holy crap" thought that went through my head as I could feel the air whisking past my face. The next thing I know I'm lying on the grass on my back next to the street looking up at the sky. It was strangely silent, almost as if I had died and was quickly ascending to heaven. Then all of a sudden the silence was broken when the guys started gathering around me and looking down. One said, "Oh my God, I can't look at it!"

Another was looking at my right leg and said he felt like he was going to puke, while the third was yelling that someone needed to go get my mom — it looks bad!

Up until this point I must have been in shock because I felt nothing. But then I looked down at my leg and between my knee and ankle it looked like I had another knee that was allowing the bottom part of my leg to bend outwards towards the street. That's all it took and suddenly the pain was intense. So intense that I felt like crying but I couldn't. I think I was past the crying point of pain and into the screaming bloody murder point. I let out a blood curdling yell and while I didn't really curse back then I dropped at last 20 f-bombs in a row while screaming to get someone to call the paramedics.

The pain was so intense that I thought I was going to either piss or crap in my pants from doing the push down with the abdomen while contorting the face and clenching the fists method to quell the pain. Wasn't working so well as it was throbbing with each heart beat and seemed to be getting sharper and hotter with each passing moment.

By now the folks who lived around the area started to come out of their houses. One woman said she called the paramedics and put a coat over me asking who my parents were. My buddy who stayed behind with me said the others went to get my mother. The crowd gathered and were trying to console me when my mom arrived. She tried to pick me up but I was too heavy plus the pain was God-awful — I was like, "Stop! Don't move me! It hurts!"

She backed off but stayed by my side until the ambulance pulled up with lights flashing and siren blaring. A police car came too and together they loaded me onto the stretcher, slid me into the back and off we went to the hospital. I thought I would be in trouble because they had to cut my Toughskins off. They couldn't be repaired, and there was no way they were going to be replaced. Rather than disown me, my mom stayed overnight with me in the hospital.

Even the most cold-blooded person has sympathy at times, so she was the mom she needed to be, at least for a couple of days. In time, though, I remember being confused as usual, when she became frustrated, having to cater to me. The "I love you," "I hate you," situation is difficult, especially for a teenager.

My wife Stacey says I'm rare, especially for a guy, because I'm not a complainer, nor do I look for sympathy when I'm hurt or sick. I can deal with it myself. It's a nuisance or an inconvenience, and I may cuss and overreact at first, but then I move on. There are too many things to accomplish in life to get bogged down. Sometimes, I slip up and tell my own children they need to "toughen up and deal with it," but I try to be conscious of that.

I had a spiral, corkscrew break in my tibia (shinbone) that had to be screwed back together. It was so bad that they had to put me to sleep to set it, living up to my favorite motto, "Go big or go home," that I still live by, and is normal vernacular for my own kids.

Instead of the normal six to eight week healing process, I needed a full leg cast for six weeks, and a half cast from the knee down, for another four. To add insult to injury, spring was in full swing, and summer was right around the corner.

Being out of commission that long gave me a lot of time to ponder my future. That spring and early summer changed the whole game for me — that shy, quiet kid was transformed, and all those close to me will tell you, he never looked back.

Until then, I was an overweight kid with buck teeth and a haircut that was the result of parents trying to save money by cutting their child's hair themselves, despite having no experience. Moms and dads, please take heed of the haircut lesson here. It never really turns out well without proper training. I wore heavy, old-fashioned "Coke bottle lens" glasses, where the person's eyes appear to bug out at you when you look at them.

I wasn't a chick magnet. Instead, I was fodder for bullies, as I was just the kind of kid they loved to feast on. I was used to being bullied at home, so it was easy to cope with. It was just another day for me.

When I broke my leg, for some reason, self-motivation took over, saying, "I am done with this. After my leg heals, things are going to be different. I am going to take control of my life, and never willingly relinquish the upper hand again, especially to a bully."

I have since learned there are times you have to relinquish the upper hand, to keep the peace, but back then, none of that mattered.

My parents didn't particularly like this, mainly because they were unable to control me like they were used to doing. But I made up my mind to change.

In eighth grade, I was transferred to Mead Junior High in Elk Grove Village, which had just been built. A new school meant new faces, and a completely different environment, the perfect set-up for a new Tom.

I started taking care of my looks. As people noticed, and reacted differently, my self-confidence grew. I lost weight, my braces melted away the buck teeth and I got contact lenses. I went from being a nerd to someone that girls started paying attention to. That sort of ego boost goes right to your head, making your whole thought process go astray. Oh, the power women have over men.

I had always played baseball, but I started to play football, for the first time. Wrestling followed shortly after, and I became a three-sport athlete. I became outwardly more aggressive, and once I realized I could take my anger out on other guys and be rewarded for it, instead of getting in trouble, I learned to really love wrestling, and especially football. The pain you can inflict is ten-fold and the pain you endure is the same. The saying it "hurts so good" resonated with me. Maybe I felt I deserved it, as that is what I was always told.

There was an Elk Grove travel football team, categorized by weight classes. Most of those in the group where I started were my age, or a year younger, with at most, only one year of experience under their belt. In order to stay in this group I had to lose 12 to 15 pounds.

After eight weeks of hardcore practices, I was selected as starting tail back and linebacker, but was devastated at the pre-season weigh-in, when I was one-point-two pounds too heavy, and they forced me to the next weight class, away from the only team I knew. I was the smallest and the youngest there, didn't play much, and eventually quit before the season ended.

The next year, I went out for football, wrestling and baseball at James B. Conant High School in Hoffman Estates, Illinois. I'm sure it's because I was stubborn and always believed I knew best, nobody took me under their wing and showed me the way. I had to figure things out for myself, mostly by trial and error. I was the new kid, so I had to be tough, down to the core, to be noticed, and break into the inner circle of athletes. But I was ready for the challenge.

Sports played a big role in my life, until junior year, when I experienced the biggest Bummer and yes, that is with a capital B. After a career ending sports injury, I could not get that aggression out through wrestling and football anymore, so I had to look for other ways.

I started working, and began to love the money, but became bored, so the socially unacceptable, rebellious behavior reared its ugly head. An extreme personality crept in, gradually taking over my persona.

My inner, secondary self took over, telling my outer self to change. I figured I had things under control and that things would work out, but I don't think I ever stopped to think about who I was becoming.

I began to become a little more popular and, as you see with the troubled young adult stars with their faces plastered all over the news, when you let popularity get to your head, out-of-control behavior is around the corner. It's just on a much larger scale for famous people.

I equate my senior year to a rock star's life of sex, drugs and rock 'n' roll. While I didn't start using drugs and alcohol until the end of high school, they seemed to make my extreme personality bubble to the surface.

My life began to spiral making each day exceedingly more exciting than the day before. Some will argue that the "spiral" was an out of control spiral but I disagree. How could I be spiraling out of control but yet maintain good grades? Maybe grades were my moral compass. Right, wrong or indifferent, I had a heck of a lot of fun, especially when alcohol was involved.

Academically, I did the least amount possible to succeed at the 110 percent level. I never glossed over anything nor did it half-assed out of fear. I prioritize extremely well, and quickly shine the best light on any situation, so I am able to accomplish 250 things when there is only time for three. My perfectionism and my socialite side were both satisfied.

I became an extrovert, but with introvert qualities and mannerisms. I think I still looked at myself as that husky, bullied, four-eyed kid that girls ignored. Even today, although I'm almost always "on," I sometimes get that feeling of low self-esteem, becoming that quiet kid again. I can't explain why, but it has a certain comfort and familiarity, resorting back to this state of active passivity. I have to consciously strive to overcome it.

I still have underlying introvert characteristics. While it's not shyness, I might find myself just sitting back and taking in the conversation before I make a comment or do anything to draw attention to myself. It's as though I feel compelled to have to know everything about what I'm going to discuss before I can say the first word. I have a deep rooted fear of criticism, of what I say, how I say it and how I look when I say it. But it has never stopped me.

Until recently, I never set goals. In my mind, it was better to achieve something and then next time, one up what I did, with no end goal, except to do as much as possible with the time I have. Some would say that's a goal, but it really isn't. Once I was able to do something, I just wanted to do more, no matter what it was. I wanted more excitement, more danger, more exhilaration or "more" anything, so long as it was more.

Maybe it's because, until junior high, I always took last, or nearly last, or maybe it's because I was beaten down by those who were supposed to pick me up. Regardless, my attitude changed to believe I could do everything well, and beat everyone and anyone at it. I thrived on competition and was filled with glory when I won, which became more common as I got older, stronger and wiser in the "street smart" sense.

Initially, I tried to impress people by bullying the bullies, being the tough guy, the daredevil, or the extremist that awed people with stupid antics, but that was not where it was at, and didn't garner the right kind of attention. I learned to be more authoritative and take more control of situations. I enjoy being the center of attention, but I'm not the annoying type who always has to have the limelight. There's a fine line. I would rather naturally influence people, by doing what the world would want me to do, and be someone that people would want to follow. I want them to see that I speak intelligently and can think on my feet. It was not until recently, especially following the shock of losing Cal, that I started to do these things.

I do very well in my insurance brokerage business and started what has become a successful charity at the same time. I just keep going, and in my mind, I have no option other than to succeed at everything. One of the rewards is the ability to give my family things I always wanted growing up. But don't get me wrong, material things are not the most important and you shouldn't live your life for them or give them to your kids without expectations.

When people see the positive transformation of going from one extreme to the other with Cal's death and Cal's Angels, it draws attention, and influences people in the right way. I keep trying to find more ways to do this. That is change that really means something.

For example, many people have lost their faith in God. If anyone should have lost faith in God, it should have been me. I lost a little at first, but not for long. Through all of this, I continue to seek God. I believe there is a master plan here for goodness, and everything functioning cohesively to bring that goodness to others.

Through all of this, my inner circle of friends never changed much, though the second tier has definitely grown. I try to be there for all of my friends as a positive influence. My friend from second grade, and my roommate from college are still my two best friends. We may not hang out all the time, but there is a connection there that no distance or lifestyle difference can change.

Some people feel uncomfortable around me, because I lost my kid. They don't know what to say or how to act, so they steer clear, as a way out of facing it with me, and for me. As I have learned, there are some people you just cannot be friends with. You can be an acquaintance, but not a "friend," for the true meaning of friend is accepting each other as you are.

My instinct is still to be an introvert, but if I get myself revved up, I can become an extrovert in the blink of an eye. I guess you could say I am an introvert by nature and an extrovert by choice.

I was shy and quiet when I was young. Today, I have dreams and aspirations of becoming a great speaker, influencing people to be the best they can be, no matter what crap life has thrown at them. And it all began with a broken leg.

CHAPTER FOUR TAKEAWAYS — DISCUSSION TOPICS

- **What "shocks to the system" have changed your life?**

- **Can you really change your core personality traits and behaviors?**

- **Have you ever experienced your "other self?" If so, describe it.**

- **Is it better to be an extrovert or an introvert? Can you be both?**

ATTITUDES:
- **Are there direct correlations between fearlessness, lack of common sense, and injuries?**

- **Is it sometimes wise to relinquish the upper hand to others? If so, when?**

- Is perfectionism learned behavior? If so, why do people become perfectionists?

- Is setting goals important?

- Do you set goals? If so, how do you set them and measure the results?

- Is setting out to outdo what you did last a real goal?

- Which is better, book smart or street smart?

RELATIONSHIPS:
- What are important qualities effective leaders must possess?

- Compare and contrast a friend and an acquaintance.

- Contrast a friend vs. an acquaintance.

CHAPTER FIVE
Putting the Extreme Personality
to Good Use

"If you ain't first you're last."

Ricky Bobby
Played by Will Ferrell in Talladega Nights

For reasons known and unknown I developed an extreme personality after that broken leg. To me an extreme personality is one that goes beyond the norm for any given situation. Most rational, cautious folks with safety in mind would not push the extreme. It is pushing the line and going over the edge without regard for injury or acknowledging the possibility of death.

When I say I have an "extreme personality" it used to mean one thing when I was younger and what some would refer to as "stupid" or being "young and stupid." I thrived on chaos and danger; I didn't believe I could or would get hurt, but this wasn't my attitude 100% of the time. There were times when I would go back to that shy kid who wanted to blend in with the woodwork. There was never anything in the middle — it was always one or the other.

This just happened without me being aware of it. One day I realized that I wanted to be a different person and push the limits to places I never did before. It is interesting how you can go from one level to another and not consciously be aware of it. It's a subconscious frame of mind that, even today when I notice I'm complacent and not getting much done, I can easily kick into high gear and when I do it's lights out. I believe I push the limit to make things more interesting, liven it up and make life exciting.

What I see differently is that I love to win and see what comes with winning. I am not a poor sport, but I am disappointed when I do not succeed. In business, my process in accepting defeat is to first look for my faults. If I made any mistakes I write them out, ponder them and guarantee myself it will never happen again. When I cannot find fault in what I did I make it easy to accept it. I spin it into their loss because, "now you do not have me as your insurance guy; your loss, not mine." This may sound a little big headed but the reason is that I truly know, deep down, that I care about my clients' insurance programs as if they were my insurance program — I do for them what I would do for myself and nothing but the best is expected with nothing left to question. I strive to do the best job possible for every single client. The care, passion and determination I put in to every insurance program are the best in the marketplace so why wouldn't I feel it really is their loss?

My drive to win and all that comes with winning allows me to peel back the layers of each defeat and figure out what to either do differently so that the same loss never happens again. I'll be the first to admit that I love to win but I stop before the "at all costs" phrase comes into play. A smart, ethical player always comes out on top in the long run.

I always strive for perfectionism in everything I do, a trait I credit to my upbringing and the high stakes expectations constantly laid out before me. While it started as a pain avoidance mechanism, I believe it shows what kind of person I am to the people I deal with in all areas of my life. This level of perfectionism is especially required if you are not there in the room with your end product; now it has to perform and sell itself without your input or assistance.

I may not be the smartest guy in this business but I will outwork anybody because I have an innate ability to survive on very little sleep and still be ready and rarin' to go on a moment's notice.

Some would think it's the sugar-free Red Bull I drink, but that is more to help me bring my thoughts back into focus once they get scattered around in my head like a deck of cards strewn about after a bad day at the poker table, than speed my system up. On more than one occasion I have had a full can a half hour before falling asleep and still got a full five or six hour night's rest — very typical for those of us with Attention Deficit Disorder.

Having ADD did not hit me until my daughter started struggling in school. After countless battles with trying to get her to complete all her homework or even turn it in when it was completed, multiple conferences with teachers and counselors because she was struggling to pay attention in class, we decided to take her to the doctor to see what's up. Turns out she has ADHD without the hyper, or H, component. When I was young, you were considered unruly or a nuisance in class, then it turned into ADD and then they added ADHD, but now I'm told they have combined the two into one category, further describing the H portion of it as being included or excluded.

All I know is I took the same ADHD diagnostic test as my daughter did and it turns out I have ADHD with a minor touch of the "H" component. I further learned from the doctors that caffeine and stimulants have a different effect on those of us with ADHD than the rest. Stimulants can result in increased focus and have a calming effect rather than speeding up the system, causing jitters and sleepless nights. I just think it's crazy how I figured out how to self-medicate on my own without even being a doctor. Red Bull is my "drug of choice" and works for me but it may not for you, it's a trial and error thing which I will not put my stamp of approval on except to say it allows me to focus, calm down and get more things done in an hour than some can do in a day.

My daughter tried all the families of meds for ADHD and became depressed on each one of them. Through her observations of me, she has settled on Red Bull as well. Again, I'm not claiming to be a doctor or even have the ability to prescribe meds but she went from practically failing out of school to mostly A's and a couple B's — a C will pop every now and then but I am very proud of her especially since I do know her struggles.

When you look at it this way, you are always growing, learning and advancing to set yourself up to succeed in the future. That is what makes me different from many of those who want to succeed because it is not an empty drive to succeed simply because "I want to" but because I know I can when I apply my knowledge, experiences and drive into one smooth action plan.

I love the thrill of the chase and I absolutely love life itself. The extremist in me strives to get the most out of every single day which means sleeping as little as is needed to still function at a high level while performing as few remedial tasks as possible and getting them done as quickly and as perfectly as possible. However, as I get older, I have learned to slow down and listen to people much more closely than ever before. I'm upset with myself for not doing this sooner as I really love to learn from others. This is a conscious effort on my part and has gone from the "remedial task" department to a necessary and enjoyable task. People in general really are very interesting and good, bad or indifferent, I love to hear their stories especially the stories of those who are much older than I am — a lot of wisdom there that needs to be shared with all.

Now, sometimes, I will just be sitting and thinking how boring things are and that I need some excitement so I'll pick something to do that is extreme in nature and a challenge to accomplish successfully. Others will comment that it's peculiar to choose to do that certain thing at that certain moment because it will make my life difficult if it doesn't work out.

All I can do is agree that it will make my life difficult if it doesn't work out, but it is going to work out because I honestly believe I can accomplish anything and everything I put my mind to accomplishing. As Napoleon Hill says, "Whatever the mind can conceive and believe, the mind can achieve."

That is my attitude. The tougher the challenge the bigger the adrenaline rush. Sure, that sticks my neck out, but I look at where it can take me. One of my own quotes is, "Those who persevere in the face of adversity shall inherit the earth."

For as long as I can remember, until recently that is, I never had a mentor or anyone I looked up to or tried to be. I basically raised myself without true parental guidance in the sense of the term "parental guidance" and had to figure things out for myself. No one ever directly told me I would amount to much, I never had anyone tell me I could "be somebody" or "be someone" someday until I got out of college and in the business world when good fortune started to roll my way. It was then that the recognition of my successes by others made me realize I can "be" and that I do like to be noticed.

Part of the struggle with the extreme personality is to keep it controlled so that the outcomes are within reason. However, it is really thrilling when you start to do something without having any idea of what the outcome will be. It's like what Forrest Gump said: "Life is like a box of chocolates you never know what you're going to get."

The best way to explain it is that it is the excitement you get walking into a completely dark and quiet room, no lights, no one else and you can't see where you're going at all or what you'll find until you do find it. I'm drawn to this excitement like a bug is drawn to a light at night.

But just like electricity, I need to remain grounded and my wife does just that. I would say having kids does it too — their dependence on me keeps my head in the game.

And letting things get to my head? Not an issue anymore — while she is my biggest cheerleader, my wife is also my accountability partner and keeps me more grounded than anyone else. She will not let me let anything go to my head but don't get me wrong, she appreciates the results of my wins but keeps me from taking it too far as she knows there are many more wins to be had. Keeping me aware of the realities in life helps keep my extreme side in check.

My main concern with my extreme behavior was never so much about whom I was becoming but whether I would come out in one piece on the other end. When I say one piece, I don't only mean physically but mentally, emotionally and spiritually as well. I still get that youthful feeling of invincibility now and again but then I am humbled by all the things good in my life that God has provided for and God has taken from me.

I guess you could say God keeps me in check.

I never realized the magnitude of my faith until everything started to develop with Cal's All-Star Angel Foundation. My yardstick of what I do and how I do it is "WWCD": What Would Cal Do? I use that not because I compare him to Jesus but because he was such a caring person.

I try to run Cal's Angels like Cal ran his life. Caring about others and putting them first before anything else. I try to live my life to be there for others and it is so fulfilling that I cannot even begin to explain it and what I get out of the whole experience. I just wish I could go back in time to my younger years and live life this way but that is not an option so all I can do is make the best of it on a forward moving basis.

Writing this book is my giveback to so many others. For the folks just figuring out what path they want to follow and what it is that will help them feel fulfilled on every level. For those who have experienced pain, suffering and adversity I'm hoping it will serve as inspiration to carry on and not give up.

And most importantly for those who have been there for me every step of the way — may this book serve as proof that none of what you supported was in vain or a waste of your time. It is all so exciting to me because I love helping people and I want to be there for others. Most of those who knew me "back when" are confused by where I'm at in my journey.

Up until Cal passed away, I lived for me and everything else slotted in below. Mr. Type A personality to the nth power has now split up that energy and applies the first segment of it to helping others and being there for them including my own family. My order of priorities has gone from me, me, work, either me again or family (not real sure which one goes where out of these two), work again then God to now being God, family, work, me.

It all goes back to when I was laying there in bed with that broken leg in seventh grade; I had a lot of time to think. I looked inward and back out and determined that I did not like my life the way it was. That was the conscious part. The part to be extreme was not conscious, that sort of and still does, just happens and comes out of left field. It's like a switch gets flipped, then watch out world, except now it's watch out world in a good way!

Some of my readers here may remember the television show, 'The Six Million Dollar Man'. Steve Austin was severely injured in the crash of an experimental Lifting Body aircraft and is "rebuilt" in an operation that costs six million dollars. His right arm, both legs and the left eye are replaced with bionic implants that enhance his strength, speed and vision far above human norms: he can run at speeds of 60 mph (97 km/h), and his eye has a 20:1 zoom lens and infrared capabilities, while his limbs all have the equivalent power of a bulldozer. He uses his enhanced abilities to work for the OSI (Office of Scientific Intelligence) as a secret agent. I always wanted to be him — he always won and was in the spotlight but that was just a dream for that chubby kid with buck teeth and glasses.

Speaking of buck teeth, I can remember my mom calling me "Bucky" and poking fun at my glasses; sick to think that actually happened but I'm guessing it was her way of trying to get me to change. Maybe that's why I push so hard — maybe I owe her a big ol' THANK YOU rather than an expression of disbelief.

After I came out of my shell and the extreme personality kicked in after breaking my leg, the drugs and alcohol are what put me over the edge and turned me into a troublemaker. I honestly cannot figure out what happened — did I always have this sort of behavior in me? Did my inner self just need a push? Was it my mom's cutting words? I don't really know but I must have always had an addictive personality and being addicted to winning came around the time my leg healed and I have never looked back.

Sometimes, however, an extreme personality left unchecked and left to run rampant and free can get you into serious trouble. In my case it was a culmination of events and repeated offenses that landed me in jail. Nothing, in my opinion, serious like murder, rape, theft, larceny or any felonies — simple craziness and out of control need-to-win while teaching people a lesson on who to mess with and who not to mess with "stuff."

While it wasn't really jail as what first comes to mind, but rather work release detention without a chance to actually leave for work at the County jail. It was still being locked up during which I had time to figure out how to stay in the game as much as possible and not get in trouble yet still cause trouble.

In other words, tread the line of right and wrong but know to be cautious and aware of where the line of legality is written. That is how I looked at things at that point in my life — a little messed up? Yeah, you could say that without much fear of being wrong.

Sure. Sometimes I daydream and want to go back and start over, have a simple life without all the responsibilities. But then I think, "Nah, this is too exciting! I'd be quite bored without the chaos of it all coming at me at once and, most of all, I wouldn't have my awesome family."

You know, I sometimes think that God did not allow me to win the lottery or make it some other way on easy street because He feared I would have done nothing with what I have in the way of giving back. All of the people in my life and I have so much to give back to help others none of which would have happened if I had fallen into the "easy life," so to speak.

Even if I would have given back it never would have been giving back in the same way I now do with Cal's Angels. If this is all true, I think He's wrong but who knows if my priorities still would have changed if I had the easy life before Cal passed?

All of this served as a big life shaper for who I am today, especially being in sales. If I had stayed that shy overweight kid with buckteeth and thick glasses, I would most likely not be in sales. I also probably would not know what it's like to break any laws especially those put in place to correct out of control behavior. But my extreme personality added a new component to the game — a big fear of the law and breaking the law and what happens when you are oblivious to the consequences of your own actions.

Time has changed me. Life experiences have changed me.

What do I think of myself?

What does God think of me now?

Can I wake up in the morning, look at myself in the mirror and know that everything I did was right — that everything I did is how I would want and expect others to treat me?

How does the public look at me?

How do they interpret my actions and reactions to situations?

Can they trust me as their insurance agent protecting their future, their wealth, their livelihood and their family if I am out causing trouble?

… That's an emphatic NO!

Can they trust me with their donations to Cal's Angels and all that Cal's Angels stands for if I am out causing trouble?

… HECK NO!

So I look at it from moral, ethical and religious viewpoints:

- WWCD: What Would Cal Do?

- WWJD: What Would Jesus Do?

- WWGD: What Would God Do?

- WWGT: What Would God Think? Of me if I did this? Is this a Godly thing to do? Am I leading a Godly life? Losing Cal made me realize a lot of things in life, especially that there is a supreme being who is in control — it's not me, it's not you … it's God and He is the one to whom I must answer.

I ask myself a lot of questions:

- How do I keep all this in balance?

- Would Cal be proud of me and what I am doing at this moment?

- Does what I do at the moment honor God?

It's pretty simple — if the answer is no, I don't do it. If the answer is yes, then I will do it. There are no grey areas — there are no in-betweens. It's a "yes" or it's a "no."

This is how I keep myself within the boundaries of life. Not an easy task in any sense of the word for one with an extreme personality but a task that is necessary and once mastered allows me to carry on. For I know that if those I report to approve of my actions and/or inactions, then I will know I am a person of good character and morals. I know I will be able to look at myself in the mirror and say, "I always did the best I could possibly do in every situation and through every circumstance. I never did anything to anyone I would not expect done to me. I treated everybody the way I would want to be treated and in the way I think they should be treated."

Therefore, I have no qualms about what I have done. That is the action you take. Sounds simple but it is not. Those are the things that go through my head for every action or reaction that comes my way. I take the time to think things through because my knee-jerk reaction is not always the best. Some may think I'm a slow decision maker or don't understand — reality is I'm taking the time to weigh all options and always trying to do what's best for everyone in my life.

CHAPTER FIVE TAKEAWAYS — DISCUSSION TOPICS

- Can you look yourself in the mirror and be happy with who it is you see looking back at you?

- What's your definition of an Extreme Personality?

PLAYING THE GAME:

- Discuss Napoleon Hill's quote: "Whatever the mind can conceive and believe, the mind can achieve."

- Are you a poor sport if you're disappointed when you lose?

- How do accountability partners keep you grounded?

PERSPECTIVES:

- Parents' comments can scar for life but can negative comments develop positive results in all aspects?

- Can winning the lottery or having the "easy life" prevent one from doing what is they were meant to do in life?

CHAPTER SIX
Coming to Terms With Your Predestination

"The mystery of human destiny is that we are fated, but that we have the freedom to fulfill or not fulfill our fate: realization of our fated destiny depends on us. While inhuman beings like the cockroach realize the entire cycle without going astray because they make no choices."

Clarice Lispector
The Passion According to G.H.

The third event that shaped who I am today was coming to an understanding of predestination or, as some call it, fate. While most of you may not consider this to be an event, I do because of the significant impact it has had on my life.

This understanding has allowed me to fully realize that the events in my life have served as a training program for what I am now doing with

Cal's Angels. None of it was clear until I got to the point where I could understand and believe that it is supposed to be this way. The toughest thing any parent will ever have to deal with is the loss of their child — all the while trying to understand why.

Then you have all the questions about God:

What God would take a child?

Why my child?

Is God punishing me?

Is it payback?

Why? Why? And Why? Again ...

You try to come to terms with all of it, but it's not a quick answer nor is it one that most can accept.

I have been asked by others more than once, "How can you believe in God? How can you put your faith in Him? How can you trust Him or His Word as written in the Book? What God would allow a child to suffer and die? He took your child, Tom. How can you believe?"

I tell them that God sent His only Son down here to take away the sins of the earth and He died for us and God was okay with it. How can I possibly not be okay with it? If God can do it, I can't help but think I'm supposed to do it and I truly believe that is what He wanted in this situation.

However, to get to the point I am at, with all of the things that have happened, understanding predestination is one of the big stepping stones in the process.

Just look at all of the events in my life — being raised in a chaotic, abusive environment fueled by alcohol, spinning out of control with extreme behaviors that constantly tread the line of legality, drug and alcohol use and abuse, fighting, terrible first marriage, two custody battles, dealing with others that have mental illness and on and on and on. Then stop and look at the person I have become. Looking back and understanding events, people and insight; it all plays upon itself.

It all comes down to understanding and believing in predestination. I had to come to terms with the fact that this is the way it is supposed to be and almost everything does happen for a reason. It all starts with sitting down and figuring out that reason by opening up and letting it hit you.

However, you cannot let it hit you until you can accept what you have gone through in your life. There is a pattern and process for everything and I believe that within those two variables lays the reason for pretty much everything that happens.

I found that I had to accept that reason while still believing in God, keeping my faith steadfast and believing that God would have my hand in this whole matter.

Thanks to some good friends of mine including John Davis, Doug Janchik and Bob, I've been able to understand that no matter what you do, you need to give it up to the Lord and let Him take control. He will provide the path for you to follow in order to lead a successful mental, emotional, physical and spiritual life — if that is in the plan.

There may be alternate paths that can happen in life but predestination gets you to the same end result. There is free will on the path to get there. Not everything you do in life is predetermined, but I firmly believe the end result of your life is pre-determined — will you grasp it and achieve your fate?

You will if you act on your instincts of following your predestined path rather than trying to do the opposite through human nature's natural instinct to exercise free will.

There are still some moments that seem to happen for no reason at all except to cause pain, anguish and misery in someone's life yet, underneath it all, I know there is a reason, albeit a very elusive reason. Or maybe it's because of a reason that has not yet made itself apparent.

What you need to do is get to that point I often get to and say to yourself, "It is what it is and there is nothing I can do about it, so I may as well make the best of what has happened and use it to benefit others."

That is what it is like with Cal's Angels. It happens and you just have to put your faith in God and say, "This is the way it is and this is the best I can do at this moment in this situation," then let it go and let Him guide you.

When my wife and I started to build Cal's Angels on nothing more than a hope and a prayer, we shared the idea in an e-mail with many people that simply stated, "We want to do something, we don't know what but will you help us?" From day one people jumped on board and those that get fully immersed in the Cal's Angels experience love it almost as much as we do for all the same reasons.

The end result is an awesome organization that just keeps happening and growing almost on its own but I do know who has His hand in it. There is no way we could accomplish all that we have accomplished on our own — there are only so many hours in a day and our heads are filled with only so much knowledge. We take it to that point where our efforts cannot change the intended or predestined outcome — it is the point where He does what is supposed to be done with it.

That really is my Master Plan for everything in life: Do what I think is best in any given situation and once I get to the point where I cannot force any more changes or change the outcome, I put it in God's hands to take over.

Even if you follow everything I say or the advice of others you still may never get an answer to certain things that have happened — like what happened with Cal. I may never get the true answer as to why he died at the age of 13 or why he had to suffer so long before he joined the Lord in Heaven but I think I know the answer. Look at Cal's Angels and what has been accomplished through the organization in just seven short years. We have raised over $2 million which has given us the ability to:

- Assist more than 500 pediatric cancer families through our various programs

- Sponsor two out of 23 floors at the new Lurie Children's Hospital of Chicago

- Send 12 young men to college on $10,000 scholarships each

- Provide the ability for less privileged boys and girls to participate in baseball and softball

All the while running at 90-cents of every dollar going to the cause.

Then I look at his picture in that Angels uniform with the mitt in one hand and the ball in the other and I say to myself, "I sure hope you can see what you have inspired us to create in your name, Cal!"

I will never really know the answer until I die and ask the Lord, "Is Cal's Angels the reason he died? Is this the reason for his suffering? Did everything he and the rest of our family go through happen the way it did so that this organization would be created to help so many others?"

It killed me to watch my son suffer along with everything that occurred in the relationship I had with his mother and the odd, tenuous relationship I have with my parents. I had to go through all of this to realize what makes for a good, healthy relationship. It all had to happen — it all had to take place and occur in my life, but I'm still not 100% sure why certain parts occurred the way they did.

What I do know is that all of it made me who I am today and made me realize that the answers to every "why" can be found hidden within the end result of whatever situation or set of circumstances have played out in my life.

But...

... What happens if the true answers never come?

You have to be fine with that and say, "I don't know for sure, but I think this is the answer."

I have gotten into arguments with people about there being a reason for everything. One guy whose kid was seriously ill told me he did not think there was a reason for his kid being sick and that it was a bunch of sh-- that it is happening to their family.

In our conversation I said to him, "You know what? I said the same thing until afterwards. Once it all happened and came to pass, I did realize there was a reason for it. You may not see it now, you may not see it in a year and you may never see it, but there has to be something there. You just need to find it, despite the fact that it may seem to be a fruitless search. The worst thing you can do is give up and say there is no reason for it."

I have witnessed many a friendship go south, rivalries begun or even deepened, hatred stirred up and physical altercations ensue because folks decided it was a good idea to debate religious beliefs. I can already see some of you getting your hairs up like a snarling dog coming to attack but hold on, hear me out.

You can get your little stat books out, newspaper clippings, "proof" of just about anything and come at me head on leading to a fight, if I decide to engage, but I won't, because you just can't reason with faith in religion.

It has everything to do with trust. Because of my earlier life, I have a hard time completely trusting most people. It is that love-hate tension. It is difficult but you just have to believe in something and for me, it was a complete full circle with believing in God. My journey went from believing, albeit forced believing in ways, to not believing, to back to a stronger faith than I ever had. I may not go to church much but I believe in God and thank Him every day for every blessing in my life.

You will find yourself saying, "I do not know. I can't do this on my own. I do not know what to do. I do not know why. I am just going to let you lead me down this path and I hope this path is the right path. I need your help in this. I cannot do it myself. Please help me do this."

In doing my work with Cal's Angels I have come across many people who are experiencing hardships of every variety, type and category. Some of them have figured out why and others have not.

I can tell you that the ones who have figured out the "why" are really doing some good things in many different ways. Those that have not figured it out make life very difficult for themselves as well as others in their life. They seem to purposely choose to do nothing. They sit around and feel sorry about "what life has dealt them" rather than say, "Life has dealt me a load of crap but I will take that crap and create gold nuggets for others to prosper with on every plane — mental, emotional, physical and spiritual."

Without the negatives in life your positives mean a lot less. Without mine I would never have been able to realize and appreciate all the good things in my life.

Not everybody who is doing good things for others as a result of a tragedy has figured out the "why" of the tragedy. They're following their instincts and doing what feels right, which is great, but imagine if they can come to terms with the fact that this is the "why" of it all; talk about passion infused purpose!

Understand that your life, whether filled with good or bad experiences, is the way it is supposed to be for you. What is the next thing that is going to happen and what is the end result of the actions you take? I do not like waiting for the answers; I want to see results now which is a direct byproduct of the extreme side of my personality. Patience really is a virtue and sometimes one just needs to sit back, relax and let things happen according to "The Plan" that is buried within their predetermined path in life.

This is what everyone needs to do to move forward for all of those in their lives, including themselves, to be happy, healthy and grateful for all that they have including each other. I am eager to see what the future holds. The anticipation of what's to come is extremely exciting and truly what it is all about for me.

CHAPTER SIX TAKEAWAYS — DISCUSSION TOPICS

PREDESTINATION:
• Is there a reason for everything?

• What is your definition of predestination?

• What is your definition of free will?

GOD:
• Will God guide you if you put your hand in his and trust him to lead you? How about if you have committed a serious sin, would he still lead you down the right path?

• Would the death of your child cause you to lose faith in God? How about the death of a child of anyone who is close you?

CHALLENGES:
• If you're not a parent, what is the toughest challenge you ever faced?

CHAPTER SEVEN
Championing the Bullied

"Liston is like most big bullies, if you can stay away and make him miss for a few rounds he'll get frustrated. Once you strip away that feeling of invincibility, he can be had."

Rocky Marciano
American Professional Boxer, World Heavyweight Champion
from September 23, 1952, to April 27, 1956.
The only person to hold the heavyweight title
and go untied and undefeated throughout his career.

I found myself fighting as a champion for those who were being bullied but I didn't realize this until a recent conversation I had with a fraternity brother of mine. For all of this time I had a lot of guilt about beating the crap out of a lot of people seemingly for no or little reason.

When I told this to him he quickly said, "You shouldn't feel bad about any of that. 98% of the guys you kicked the crap out of deserved it and if it wasn't you it would have been someone else. We used to sit back, enjoy the show and be happy we were on your side. I do leave that 2% margin of error in there because I'm sure some of them were a victim of circumstances rather than really deserving it."

After this conversation I was able to reflect and really get my story straightened out so that I could put it in writing. With my fraternity brother's perspective and my own observations, I've been able to look back with some clarity.

Bullying is a big topic today. I define bullying as picking on someone of a lesser physical, mental or emotional stature than yourself. There's also intimidation; taking advantage of the person by pushing them around or exerting authority over them that you may or may not have. Because bullies have the wherewithal to do it, they take advantage of it.

I come from a background of being bullied. From parental bullying to school ground bullying, I was one of the bullied. Once I entered that out-of-control phase in my life, I decided to pick on the ones who were doing the bullying. Guess you could say I decided to make a sport out of challenging the bullies to a bit of their own game and giving them a taste of their own medicine. I even went so far as to confront my friends if they started to pick on someone. I just would not allow it to continue — friend or not. I could feel the others pain because "I was there."

If I saw somebody doing the bullying and they thought they were really tough, it didn't matter how big they were, I felt it was my duty to "teach them a lesson."

I would play a little game by first asking, "Why don't you do that to me?" Funny how a bully can sense when it's coming back at them, most start to back down when it's about to come their way.

Notice I say most, there are the legitimately crazy ones who'd bring it right back at me, something I found extremely exciting back in that era of my life. The bigger, the badder, the better it was.

But those that would start to back away were also fun. They'd give you the ol' "I have no problems with you," to which I'd ask, "What if I gave you a reason to have a problem with me?"

They really didn't like that and they always seemed extremely uncomfortable as they would start to back down.

So I'd ask, "You're just what, a tough guy picking on someone you know you can handle? I'd like to see if you can handle me; what do you think?"

I would either not get a reply or, "We're just having fun," to which I'd ask, "Really? Doesn't look like he's having fun, but you know, I like having fun and want to have some fun. Do that to me. I want to see how much fun it is."

The funny thing was, as I would escalate the situation, most of them would back down because they were just bullies with nothing to back it up with. This confidence and, what I like to refer to as mind-games, seemingly ended a lot of these confrontations. But my extreme personality didn't believe in half-measures.

I had felt the pain of the other guy, so I was not going to let the bully get away with it. They started something and I was going to make them prove how tough they really were — or maybe show them just the opposite — how weak they really were; physically, mentally, emotionally and spiritually.

The bullies I really liked to challenge were the ones who pushed around women, especially the punks who controlled their girlfriends through bullying. When I witnessed this scenario playing out I couldn't help myself but to approach and start in by first asking the guy, "So what did she do? Seems like it was pretty bad."

Based on the response coupled with the associated body language, I had to quickly discern what was going on before taking the next step.

I've never hit a woman, but the sequences of a few events have resulted in me grabbing an arm pretty hard while physically restraining another from hitting and kicking me.

Because of my experience I know that in these situations emotions suddenly take over causing someone to snap, losing all self-control including the ability to reason, think clearly and see that there is just no possible way there will be a positive outcome.

Because of all this, I can see how some guys could lose it, so you have to be careful to determine the facts before figuring the manner in which you're going to come to a woman's rescue. Is it bullying, or a guy who lost it due to some inexcusable behavior on the woman's part and he now needs to be "talked down from the ledge?"

When I'd ask what she did, the verbal and associated physical response I'd get made it easy and quick to tell what was playing out. The bullies would get all tough and either ask if I had a problem or tell me to mind my own business, which kicked in the challenge response.

"Hmm, you're obviously pretty tough as I can see from how you're manhandling her. How about her and I switch places?"

The typical bully back-down would usually ensue and the rest would play out in a rather crazy manner, but again, back in those days I fed off of it. It was treading that line that made life so exciting, but ultimately dangerous.

Did I always win? Nope, but I usually won. I took every loss as a lesson to learn from and not make the same mistakes again.

I always believed, and had the attitude to go along with it, that I was not going to lose — I was always in that "ultracompetitive" mode you see with star athletes and successful business people.

My thirst for physical challenges didn't end with bullying confrontations. In college, I really wanted to get back into sports and be on the football team, so I took steroids. I was a pretty solid dude with a bit of a 'tude who was juiced up on 'roids and, at times, didn't think straight. What a combo and believe me, "roid rage" is a real thing that can be defined.

This drastic change in my physical appearance caused concern for what others, especially my parents, thought of me. All along I kept telling them how much I was working out, how taking amino acids and protein shakes was helping and how much strength I was gaining. I was trying to lessen their shock when they would eventually see me, hopefully alleviating the suspicion I was doing things I shouldn't be doing.

I left for college weighing no more than 150 lbs. and when I finally came home for Thanksgiving that year I weighed an impressive 205 with hardly any fat. I can remember trying to get in the house with no intention of discussing the weight lifting, but the door was locked, so I rang the doorbell. When my mom answered it she looked at me, eyes widened in shock with a trace of fear.

"What happened to you?" I walked in the house, she looked me up and down and said, "You look like a completely different person."

Shyly and almost embarrassed I said, "What? I told you all along I've been working out, taking my amino acids and protein powder — stuff works great!"

She quickly chimed in and said, "There's no way that's from amino acids and protein; you're taking steroids. Look at the puffiness you have going on and you have doubled in size in three months!"

"No idea what you're talking about. I gained a few pounds but that's it."

No matter what I said, she wasn't buying it and knew I was lying. Even Pop knew deep down I was taking steroids — he called me out on it many times but I just couldn't admit it to anyone.

Why am I telling you about fighting, championing the bullied, and especially about the 'roids? I know, it sounds so crazy, but from my mistakes and earlier choices I've learned to turn them into benefits. In my commercial insurance career it has taught me to never worry about who or how big the competition is for an account, because I still follow the mantra — the bigger the badder the better.

I still say, "Bring it," but in a much saner manner that doesn't leave any physical marks. This takes things to a level without the violence but yet it is a fight … it is a business fight.

From being bullied at home as a child to being bullied at school and ultimately taking care of the bullies laid the foundation for whom I am today. You could say my whole persona today is a result of going from little to no self-esteem to experiencing a life-changing event that caused me to climb the ladder to extreme self-esteem, only to be knocked down more than a few pegs after being handed the biggest smack down through the death of my oldest child, Cal.

CHAPTER SEVEN TAKEAWAYS — DISCUSSION TOPICS

BULLYING:
* Define bullying.

* What forms does it take?

* When does it occur?

PERSONAL EXPERIENCE:
* What is your experience with bullying?

* Have you ever been bullied? If so, how did it make you feel?

* Have you ever been the bully? If so, why?

* Have you ever witnessed someone else getting bullied? Did you intervene? Why or why not?

* Can businesses ever be bullies?

ATTITUDES:
* Is it ever okay to hit someone?

* Does anyone ever "deserve it?"

* Are there any life lessons in fighting?

* Can you learn from mistakes?

CHAPTER EIGHT

Jail

"What does not kill me makes me stronger."

Friedrich Nietzsche
German Existentialist Philosopher
from his highly influential Twilight of the Idols

The fourth most significant event in my life was going to jail during my college days. It was not "jail" in the classic sense. I spent nine days in the work-release department of the DeKalb County jail. It's definitely something I see as a complete oxymoron, I was not "released" but stayed put for nine days. That was more than enough to convince me that there had to be better ways to get things done.

The initial lesson I learned was different than what it is now. I now know that there are consequences for socially unacceptable actions.

Here's the lowdown as to why I went to the pokey — there was this guy I caught stealing stuff out of my room at the fraternity house. He was from the same fraternity but a different school, so he said all he was doing was trading fraternity shirts. From my perspective there were two problems with his story — he had no shirt to trade and I had no idea we were "trading" until I walked in on him.

It was a pretty pathetic scene on his part. When I caught him and pointed out the "two problems," he instantly started shooting off his mouth pretty good, which got me riled up. Then the girl I was dating at the time decided to chime in about him basically being an idiot and he said, "Shut up, fat ass," which is interesting because she was not fat at all.

Nonetheless, my instant reaction was to jack him a few times and beat him around like a rag doll. He did not fight back, but he sure kept up with the mouth. I had to put a stop to it by giving him one more shot to the noggin and he fell into the ledge on the wall knocking his front teeth out.

The cops told me that if I had only hit him in my room this probably wouldn't have been such a big deal because he was in my "house" at that point. However, the shot I gave him that sent him into the wall was in the party room on the first floor, a public space. That changed things. They deemed it to be "excessive force" and that is what got me up in front of the judge.

I can remember it vividly. After going through an actual jury trial, because I was not going to plead guilty to this one, I felt, and still feel, it was provocation — I was convicted of assault and battery. The judge then asked me to approach the bench so he could "chat" with me a bit. He asked if I was going on spring break and I said yes so he asked where. I told him Daytona and he asked with whom, how long, how we're getting there, etc. He really seemed interested, almost excited for me, so I laid out all the plans thinking wow, this judge is actually pretty cool.

Much to my chagrin, it turns out he was just messing with me with all the questions. At the height of my excitement in telling the story he interrupted and said, "I am tired of seeing you in my court room over the years so I hate to ruin your day, but you're not going on spring break — as a matter of fact, you will not be leaving the State for the next 12 months."

He then went on to ask me when my last class would end before spring break and I told him around three o'clock in the afternoon to which he replied, "Then I want you to show up at the DeKalb County Jail by 5:00

p.m. where you will stay until 5:00 p.m. on the Sunday before you go back to school."

I was shocked and thought that this isn't for real, it's a frickin' nightmare. All the scenes from the horrible movies you see on TV about why they call it the "pokey" flashed in my head — anal rape, physical abuse, gangs, the Aryan Nations, more anal rape — I was like, "Oh boy, start talking your way out of this one; there's no way this has a happy ending."

I tried explaining how I was a victim of circumstances in all the other times I was in front of him but he cut me off and said to save my breath, wished me luck and hoped that my punishment would teach me a lesson.

While my attorney at the time was unable to get me out of jail time, he was able to keep me out of the general population and not have to report until that Saturday morning. A few extra hours of freedom and I figured work-release can't be all that bad.

I remember spending that time in the county jail in a large room full of cots with anywhere from ten to 15 other guys, mostly from the local farms. I was known as "college boy" and to get the full effect, you have to say it with a semi-southern drawl with a redneck inflection.

It was spring planting time so they would go off to farm the fields in the morning then return in the evening, hammered to the bajeezus — most were in for multiple DUI's. The offences didn't faze the guards though, they all knew each other and were friends and/or related somehow. Except for me, and they made sure I knew it. Their "Hey college boy" references and the insinuations that they were going to do something to me while I was sleeping were annoying, but for whatever reason that's about as bad as it got.

Since I arrived in the morning when they were out "plantin' the taters" or whatever it is they would say in their drunk slang when they came back, I picked a cot in the corner so my back would always be against the wall.

That first night they made some disturbing comments like, "This is gonna play out like the movie Deliverance" and, "Better keep one eye open, college boy."

I told them I had no idea the locals were gay and informed them of the fact that I slept all day so I could stay up all night while they slept — maybe

I was going to be the one to get somebody after they fell asleep ... ever think about that, boys?

Of course they denied being gay and while they acted cool, the entire night they would take turns with one guy awake as a lookout for an hour at a time. Guess they weren't so sure about "college boy."

By about Wednesday or so they had "taken a likin' to college boy," but I wasn't sure if it was all a ruse to get me to let my guard down; I watched plenty of movies to know better. I continued my sleep regimen until Sunday and was gone before they came back from the fields. I had never been happier for school to start in my entire life.

After it was over my first thoughts were ones of defiance. I knew how far I could push it, what I could do and could not do, and what I could or could not get away with. I could've dragged that bastard back into my room, beat the crap out of him, kept him there, and then lie about what happened saying that he swung at me first.

That was my first thought, not real clear or real bright, and if nothing else came of this, I had a much better idea on how to cause trouble, but not pay the price — kind of a "note-to-self" deal. I can hear Forrest Gump now saying, "Stupid is as stupid does ..."

Flash forward to present and now I know it was not the right way to think. What the judge was trying to say was, "You are out of control and you need to figure out how to get yourself under control. In order to help you accomplish this, I am going to send you away for a 'learning spring break' on how to get yourself under control."

That was a shock to my system and changed the way I act and react forever.

CHAPTER EIGHT TAKEAWAYS — DISCUSSION TOPICS

- Have you ever been the victim of a crime? If so, how did you feel? What did you want to do? What did you do?

- Is "an eye for an eye, a tooth for a tooth" a great way to handle wrongs in your life?

- How do you make sure the lessons you are trying to teach to those that have committed a wrong are learned and understood the way they were intended?

CHAPTER NINE
Learning From Unfortunate Choices

*"In the long run, we shape our lives, and we shape ourselves.
The process never ends until we die. And the choices we make
are ultimately our own responsibility."*

Eleanor Roosevelt
First Lady of the United States 1933 to 1945

This is the story about how I met my first wife.

Right out of college, I started in the insurance business selling individual life insurance for Mutual of New York (MONY). I'll never forget how I got suckered into the business. I was at a Northern Illinois University job fair and was enamored with the big sign at this particular booth labeled "Financial Planning Careers."

They didn't have any trouble selling me on the concept: I was an economics major with a lot of business and finance classes under his belt so I signed up immediately. I'll never forget the first day at work. We were sitting around a rather large table in the training room listening to "the pitch" from the General Manager. Suddenly the guy next to me — a big guy who played football at Valparaiso — leaned over and nudged me. "Holy crap, dude," he said. "We're going to be schlepping life insurance."

He was right on the money. I quickly learned how to cold call, seeing as none of my friends and fraternity brothers had any money. It wasn't a whole lot of fun, but I was never an easy quitter and I was determined to make it work. I stayed with the job for 18 months. During that period — on a fateful Thursday night, known as the "hot night out" for singles back then — my life was forever changed.

There was a guy I knew and I was trying to turn him from "new friend" into "new client." He liked to hit the bars "trolling for chicks" (as he called it). He was a trust fund baby, so he didn't have many worries in life except where the fun was going to happen next. He asked me to join him for a night out. I tried as hard as I could to decline but he wouldn't have any of it. He finally convinced me. "All right," he said. "You drive a hard bargain … so if you go out tonight, I'll buy all your drinks."

Bingo. I was fresh out of college, low on cash, and still in the "party mode" phase of my life, so that offer certainly hit the right chord. We hit the road in a flash.

So, there we were at one of the hot places in town: The Safari Club in Schaumburg, Illinois. (Interestingly enough, that place has not only closed in the years past, but there isn't even a building on the property anymore.) I tried my best to have a good time, but the dance floor was the big draw of the night and I did not like to dance. As it turns out, neither did she, though I did not know it at the time when we first bumped into each other. One thing lead to another and I got her number. Soon enough we were dating.

Being a recent college grad as well as a struggling life insurance salesman with no real cash in his pocketbook to speak of, I lived in sleepy Hollow with my parents, and she lived on the opposite end of the earth in Evergreen Park, with her own parents. As the relationship grew, I moved on to the insurance brokerage world, doubled my income on day one, and before the year was done we ended up moving in together in a centrally located one bedroom apartment in Arlington Heights, Illinois.

Although details are murky, in our time spent together she had at some point ceased to take her birth control pills (whether intentionally or not). This went on without my knowledge. I only learned of the "snafu" once she told me she was pregnant.

She explained to me that she had been forgetting to take them. To make up for this, she would stack up on two per day. Shocked, I responded suspiciously. "Dang, I'm not an expert but I do know you can't play catch-up with birth control pills. Why didn't you tell me what was going on?"

She didn't have an answer for me, and insisted that it was too late to worry about any of that now. She was right: we did have to figure out what to do moving forward.

We had never seriously thought of marriage as an option. After all, a ton of well-off people have had kids without getting married — why should we have been any different? In the end, however, we finally caved in to pressure from both of our mothers. Mine was the worse of the two. She constantly badgered us with demands. She told us repeatedly that she didn't want to have a "bastard for a grandchild," that we needed to get married, that we shouldn't embarrass her … so on and so forth.

From my perspective on my mother, it was always about her and what other people thought of her if her son had a child out of wedlock. Eventually I was guilted into the marriage against my better judgment.

In November of 1992 we went to the Rolling Meadows courthouse and were married by the Justice of the Peace. Unfortunately, the relationship — even to this day — proved to be far from peaceful.

In the end I really had no way of knowing any better at the time, but "doing it the right way," as my mother put it, definitely turned out to be the wrong way. No question. I was young, naïve and uncertain of what constituted a good, healthy relationship. I was never able to witness a healthy relationship so I was flying blind into a marriage that was only going to hurt me. This decision alone cost me and others around me many years of heartache and just under a couple hundred thousand dollars in legal fees over the course of a decade.

Not all turned out bad though. In the midst of it all, we had our son Cal on June 7, 1993. Things moved along normally — or at least normal as

I understood it to be — and two years later we had our second child, Ryan, followed by our daughter Jessica in 1997.

Once we had Jessie, it hit me: I have three kids who are going to depend on me to provide for them and give them a good life. I decided to get out of "party mode" and become serious about life. I was going to work hard to give my kids everything. Most importantly, I was going to give them a father with an active role in their lives.

We were both working crazy hours in those years, just sort of barely grazing past each other during the week. The biggest exceptions were Fridays, when we had our weekly dinners as a family. Being new in the insurance business, 60+ hour work weeks were more the norm than the exception. I basically disappeared during the week from Monday through Thursday. In order to avoid daycare, she worked all weekend long. It felt important to designate Fridays — from late afternoon through dinner — as "family time."

By early 1998, the façade maintaining our marriage began to fade. I clearly remember the exact moment I knew for sure that it was over: One Friday night at our family dinner she looked at me and shot me the following stinger: "I have all I want in life. I have three beautiful, healthy children. We're all okay without you being around ... so you're free to go. All I need is money to take care of the kids."

Shocked, I thought I must have misunderstood her. She couldn't possibly have meant for me to leave for good and get out of their lives. I asked if she meant for me to go out with my friends for the night, but she clarified: "No. You're free to go out and live your life free from the burden of a family."

I didn't know how to react, so I simply left with no real direction, destination, or plan. I was alone to contemplate things. I returned several hours later and told her I wanted to make things work. I wanted to figure out how to keep the family together. Although she agreed to my plea, I now know she never truly meant to give it a fair shot and deep down I know I didn't either. I was worried about the kids growing up without an active father in their lives. I didn't want their childhoods to be like mine.

As fate would have it, a rather bizarre situation occurred in the wake our seemingly peaceful agreement. It occurred at one of the kids' family birthday parties held at our house. Both sides of the family had been invited that day, and at this point of the party things were beginning to wind down. Before the night had ended, an incident occurred and she became upset with me when I reprimanded Cal for biting his brother.

She responded violently. She hit me, kicked me, and ripped my shirt. She screamed at me from the top of her lungs, calling me every name in the book. The worst part was that the two boys — both Cal and Ryan — were stuck in the middle of it all. In the middle of her outrage, she knocked me into the boys and blamed me for it all. To this day she still says it was all my doing. Not sure why she even brings it up but she does.

This experience was a big eye-opener for me: I realized how much this situation was reminiscent of my mother's behavior when she had been drinking. My ex-wife had so many bouts like this during the course of our marriage that I couldn't help but have horrible flashbacks. She reminded me so much of my mom. I still can't get the look on my ex-wife's face out of my mind, or how closely it mirrored the look my mom often wore. When they drank like this, my thoughts of them both merged to form a fearsome, imposing figure that I would give anything not to face.

At this time, my side of the family had already left. The only ones left at the house were my ex-wife's mother and sister, but they were downstairs during the incident and unable to witness it. Their first thoughts landed on disbelief: There was no way she could have been responsible for this. There was no way this was the doing of their beloved daughter/sister. The incident had been violent and quickly spiraled out of control, and they figured it must have been my doing. I had indeed been quite loud, so it was no surprise that they called the police. By the time the officer arrived I had removed myself from the situation. I found myself outside breathing the fresh air so I could bring some sense of reality back into my spinning head.

The officer looked at me through the light from his flashlight and saw the bleeding scratches and torn shirt. He asked, in surprise, if I was alright. I told him I was and explained the events of the evening. He instantly figured my ex-wife had to be in worse shape, or that the kids might be in danger.

A half hour passed before he finally came back out and said he saw no bruises or cuts on anyone else. He asked if I wanted to file any charges and I declined, explaining that it would be embarrassing to admit that "a chick had kicked my ass." He chuckled at this, though it may have been more out of sympathy than anything else. Maybe he felt bad for me. He informed me that either I or my wife had to leave for the night in order to give everyone a chance to calm down. I called my parents to pick me up (I'd had a few beers, too, and the cop told me that neither of us could drive.)

When she learned that the cops weren't going to arrest me for domestic abuse nor press the matter any further, she got irate and warned me that this "wasn't over," even as I pulled away in the car with my dad. It felt a bit like being a kid again, getting into trouble just like I did in the good old days.

A couple days later, I discovered what she meant when she said it "wasn't over." She called DCFS and told them I had abused the kids that night. They showed up at the house while she was out with the kids, conveniently having removed herself from the situation. The DCFS investigator and I had a nice chat wherein I calmly explained how things had gone down. I conveyed as best as I could that there hadn't been any abuse, but instead a big fight that the kids had gotten dragged into. I told the investigator that these fights played out the same way on a regular basis. At some point in the next few days, he discussed things with her as well. The result was forced marriage counseling by DCFS.

Throughout the next several months, the counselors had witnessed enough and were left with only one conclusion: we didn't belong together. She had constantly stated things like, "Tom doesn't understand that he no longer matters," and, "Tom needs to take a back seat to everyone else." They told her that this line of thinking was wrong, but she never seemed to be convinced. We didn't accomplish a lot through the counseling, but we did learn for sure that we had to make a drastic change.

We both agreed to move on and get divorced. I did the paperwork and several months later, in June of 2000, I moved out. I now know it would have been a heck of a lot smarter to move out immediately, but I had no money and was forced to tough it out for four months under the same roof as her until I finally wound up living in my parents' basement. The entire process took two years, seven months and six days.

Looking back and seeing who I married for my first wife, was that an important — even good? — component of my life that shaped me into who I am today?

The answer to this question is an "indubitably so." Such a bizarre set of psychologically anguishing situations and emotionally taxing predicaments really makes one think inward and outward concerning who to blame, or if the blame belongs to both of you. I can certainly tell you it has not only made me stronger as a person but also more understanding of those suffering from mental illnesses. Many of them really cannot help doing what they do, saying what they say and living how they live.

I definitely am selective with whom I want to do business, who I keep as friends and who I choose to be in a relationship with. From point A to point Z and every point in between, you can bet your sweet bottom on the fact that I wouldn't be who I am today without the events of my first marriage.

My biggest takeaway was the realization that I had essentially married my mother on the first go-around. My son says it disturbs him to think of it that way because it makes him his grandmother's child. I know that it does sound funny to say it that way, but it really is true: I married the person who was most like my mom. It's peculiar how the natural tendency is to be drawn to what you don't like, but it just seems natural and comfortable to remain in the climate you are most used to. In this case, my climate was chaos, turmoil and instability — just like our house was when I'd been growing up.

Now, things are different. Being married to my second wife, Stacey, has driven these points home even more. I'm now happy to know that you can have a relationship defined by complete respect for each other, with no constant irritation and fighting. You can find someone and still be happy and comfortable. At times, "normalcy" still feels foreign and awkward. I'm able to push through that hesitation and see that it's actually a pretty cool feeling.

It helps, too, in searching for new sales people in my line of work at the insurance agency. One hire I chose on my own turned out to be one of the best inexperienced "newbies" we have ever had employed at the agency. I've been able to focus on what makes people successful and work with them to achieve their success, starting with leading by example. I do it at the insurance agency, with Cal's Angels and in life in general.

I've dedicated myself to preventing people from making the same mistakes I did. I definitely made a lot of them along the way. While some would say all I needed to do was wizen up and make better choices, I will tell you that it's not as easy as it sounds. It's even harder when your basic instincts were instilled within you from early childhood, and those instincts draw you to chaotic situations. I've been through several personal hells on Earth at times, but when you're on the back end of it all, reflecting on everything that has occurred before, suddenly it's crystal clear. You finally know what to do, and especially what not to do.

CHAPTER NINE TAKEAWAYS — DISCUSSION TOPICS

- When something goes wrong in your life is it ever okay to blame someone else? In my case, I could blame the guy who lured me out with the promise of free drinks that fateful night I met my ex-wife. Should I or could I hold a grudge?

RELATIONSHIPS:
- Should parents influence their children's choices when they are adults? How about as young children under their roof?

- What are your thoughts about women being attracted to men who are like their fathers and men being attracted to women who are like their mothers?

- What makes for a strong family unit in your opinion?

PERSPECTIVES:

- What is normal?

- Can what most would consider to be normal actually feel abnormal to some?

- Is it easy to twist the facts of a situation and make it look entirely different?

- Are men automatically assumed to be the aggressors in physical altercations? If so, why?

- Is vindictiveness a sin? How about a sign of mental illness?

- At what point should you start to take life seriously?

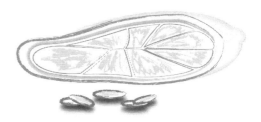

CHAPTER TEN
Need to Grow Up Fast? Have a Child...

"Having children is like living in a frat house - nobody sleeps, everything's broke and there's a lot of throwing up."

Ray Romano, American Actor,
Stand-Up Comedian, Screenwriter and Voice Actor

Having kids changes your whole outlook on life, or at least it should. It has had a major impact on my life in more ways than, not just one, but probably a hundred or two.

I married my first wife because I was instinctively drawn to the wild, seemingly untamed and chaotic edge to her. She married me because I was a "bad boy." One of those extremely odd sort of comments she made to the counselors was, "I married a bad boy and wound up with a love sick pussy."

The counselor said, "You have kids, a family and need to take life seriously," to which she shot up so fast and forcefully that she almost fell forward out of her seat when she snapped back, "No, it's not a good thing! You're only saying this because you're a guy and on his side."

I've always felt that he was right and she was wrong, but there was no changing her mind on a topic like this.

After Cal was born, I could see myself undergoing a change. My transformation made me into a man who took his career, his family and his own life more seriously as each of my three kids were born. My first wife tried to change, and even appeared to have changed, until somewhere along the way after Jessie was born a "normal life" got the best of her.

She decided she didn't want to be married — she just needed money to take care of the kids and started living the life only a bad boy could love and this bad boy had left the building.

Towards the end of our marriage her work shift changed to evenings ending around midnight or later. I can remember many times being ready to roll out the door for work at 5:00 in the morning but having to wait on the stairs for her to come rolling in. Her excuse was always the same — she went out after work and fell asleep in her car. I knew it was a lie but I didn't care anymore — I just needed to get out and move on with my life while trying to maintain plenty of contact with my children, so they knew who their father was and that I loved them.

Having children is right there with the top significant things in my life because it forced me to grow up, take things more seriously, become an adult, a parent and mature beyond the forces that were trying to hold me back in my quagmire of mediocrity and insignificance.

CHAPTER TEN TAKEAWAYS — DISCUSSION TOPICS

RELATIONSHIPS:
- Why are some women drawn to the "bad boy?"

- Why are some women drawn to the "lovesick pussy?"

- Which is better?

- Is there a middle ground or balance between the two that is ideal?

- Do children change your life? If so, how?

CHAPTER ELEVEN
My Cal — Part 2

"To become a father is not hard,
to be a father is, however."

Wilhelm Busch
German Humorist, Poet, Illustrator and Painter

O n June 27, 1995 we welcomed our second child. I kind of got my way in naming him too, but not really. One of my other favorite baseball players was Ryne Sandberg from the Cubs. His mom made me settle on Ryan while using my middle name for him — Ryan Michael Sutter. Still a cool name but I knew he was going to have to try harder because of the name change late in the game. Child number three came on August 15, 1997 and I was not allowed to have anything to do with her name because she was a girl. I still love her name though — Jessica Renee Sutter. All three of my kids turned out to be great athletes and if you ask their mother, it's because they take after her. There is no way they take after me because I was an overweight, bucktoothed, four eyed little wuss boy who was bullied, so how could they have any of those genes in them she asked. "Whatever" was quickly becoming my favorite thing to say to her at this point.

Cal picked up on baseball rather quickly and became "one of those kids" every coach wants on their team. He batted lefty, threw righty, pitched and played center field with the ability to throw kids out at the plate from deep center field when he was only 10 years old. He was fast and developed a knack for leadership even quicker. Even though he was a great athlete and always in the top three on his team, he never let it get to his head. He lead by example, never put anyone down and was as good of friends with the top kids as he was with the last kid on the list. This is why his last coach called him "Cal Man", because he was a man in a kid's body.

Cal dabbled in other sports like soccer. That didn't last long especially when he learned the real rules after his first game. A kid made a break down the sideline with the ball and Cal came across the field on a diagonal running full speed right at him. As he got closer all I could say to myself was, "Oh no, he's going to take that kid out!"

And he did!

Rather than go for the ball, Cal leveled him with a full on body shot. The kid hit the ground and you could hear that total exhale sound someone makes when the air gets knocked out of them.

As the kid lay there wheezing in an effort to catch his breath, the crowd let out a gasp in disbelief at what just happened. I could hear a couple ask whose kid that was. I pretended like I had no idea and even acted like I didn't approve of it either in an attempt to hide my identity. However, on the inside, the guy part of me was like, "Yes, that's my boy who just laid your boy out like a sack of potatoes!"

All the while this was going on, Cal took the ball and started going towards the goal as the ref was blowing the whistle trying to get him to stop. He looked back over his shoulder with one of those "who me?" looks on his face and when he realized it was him, he stopped.

We were eventually both figured out and most of the parents had this uppity attitude that they didn't want us involved if we were going to display such violence. I tried to explain how he didn't know any better and that he was just being competitive in a sport similar to the one the neighborhood boys played in the front yard called soccer-football. It fell on deaf ears and after the season was over we never returned to soccer … ever.

Cal continued to play baseball and further fell in love with the game. He was able to be competitive, but not so much that he got hurt. Turns out he didn't like violence all that much. He tried football on a trial basis because they thought he might be a good quarterback with the arm he had in baseball. He didn't last more than a week after getting his clock cleaned a few times.

I can remember one instance during his battle with cancer where his competitive side really showed through. We were at our house and he started to spike a fever. For those not familiar with the cancer fight, once the fever starts to spike you need to get into the emergency room — especially when it's a child.

When we left the house he was at 102 or so and by the time we got to the hospital, after two hours fighting rush hour traffic to downtown Chicago, he was getting close to 105. Still not much to worry about as fevers that high were commonplace. However, as the night wore on the fever kept climbing even though they were loading him up with the meds. As it hit 106.5 I started calling his mom, but couldn't reach her. I left several voice mail messages about the situation and that he may not make it.

I was worried and started to think the worse as he started to hallucinate. First he was a knight telling me the sword was piercing his armor, then there were rainbows and other crazy things. They kept loading him with meds and pumping in the IV fluids but the fever now was over 107 — he was on all fours throwing up blood and I was praying to God to please take me, not him, he's too young. I called his mom again and no answer still. I called Stacey and she talked me down from panic mode. I couldn't handle this and now he's puking blood — my kid is dying!

The last reading they had was 107.9 and then it started to fall, very slowly — oh thank God. Within a few hours they had us up in the ICU and I finally passed out knowing his fever was controlled at 103 and still falling.

About 8:00 a.m. I was lying on the bed that was lower and on the left side of his bed when I heard this faint voice in my dreams saying, "Hey Dad, you up?"

I slowly came to my senses and opened my eyes to Cal's face looking down at me and he said, "I have to pee, can you help me?"

It was like a dream at first — you go from thinking your kid is dying to seeing him talking normal, first thing when you wake up. I said, "Of course I can help but first, how do you feel?"

He told me he was fine and remembered nothing. All I could think of is how this was some crazy stuff.

After he peed we laughed about how high the fever was and the crazy hallucinations that ensued. When the doctors came to check on him he asked what was the record for the highest fever ever that someone survived. They said they didn't know offhand and asked why.

He proudly said his was 107.9 and wanted to know where it ranked. They did some checking and informed Cal from what they could tell that he held the record. He let out a triumphant "Yesssss" and high fived me.

I could tell the docs weren't sure if that was something to be proud of but they went along with it. We did finally find his mom later the next day and she spoke to him by phone. He told her all about it and gauging from his reaction, I'm guessing she wasn't all that impressed with his triumphs.

When Cal relapsed in the early winter of 2006, we were sent down to St. Jude's for a consultation which resulted in a stem cell procedure using unrelated and low matched donors. After that didn't work and all of the docs within the current system of providers gave up, I sent out a plea to my circles. Through various contacts and many phone consults, we wound up at the University of Minnesota Hospital in an experimental program. At each one of these facilities, Cal was sure to tell them all about his 107.9 fever, then asked if anyone there ever beat his record. From the responses it seemed like he was the winner and very lucky to be alive without any brain damage.

It was this competitive nature that made him so good at baseball and it was the feel of the game where he could lose himself, putting all his worries behind him for the moments he was on the field.

As competitive as Cal was, he was also extremely sensitive with a lot of feelings and cared for others more than any other young man I have ever known, especially a young man who was a great athlete.

A perfect example of this was already mentioned in how his coach called him "Cal Man" because of the way he treated his teammates — he was a man in a kid's body. Cal was always in the top three on the team and it didn't matter if it were the best kid on the team or the least talented kid on team, in Cal's eyes they were all his teammates and his friends. If the others started picking on the number 13 out of 13 guy, Cal would go out of his way to make sure he felt welcome. This display changed the others' attitudes and you could see them drop their childish behaviors towards their teammate. Not sure what they were thinking, but I'm guessing it was something along the lines of — if he's good enough for Cal to be friends with, he's good enough for me.

Now, there may be one guy who disagrees with this whole "sensitive, thoughtful young man" thing and that would be his brother Ryan who is two years younger.

They loved each other as much as any brothers do but they also could fight worse than any brothers do. Ryan knew exactly how to get to Cal and get him aggravated. The last big fight I remember was when Cal was in the midst of his battle with cancer. They were playing Xbox — I believe Madden NFL — and Cal was whooping him. Ryan kept agitating and agitating so Cal cracked him in the head with the controller. It was such an impactful wallop that I heard it upstairs from the basement.

Instantly Ryan came running upstairs bawling while holding his head and could barely say how Cal had hit him in the head because he was hyperventilating. I had not seen the start of it so I went downstairs where Jessie and Kiley had witnessed the whole debacle. Both instantly chimed in saying how Ryan was taunting Cal by standing up over him, calling him names like loser, stupid and dummy while adding in how he was going to hurt him. As Ryan sat back down Cal took the controller and cracked Ryan hard right in the side of the head.

Part of me wanted to tell Ryan he deserved it but I didn't. I took the middle road and said that while I know Ryan is aggravating and extremely annoying, we still don't hit and especially don't hit someone in the head with an Xbox controller. I also told Ryan he needs to think about what he's doing because one day Cal, or someone else he does this to, will end up really hurting him.

During the divorce process, Cal and Ryan decided to join Cub Scouts and I took the reins in being the parent who did it with them. I was never a Scout so it was pretty cool doing all those projects: Going camping, learning about nature and making new friends. The one and only year we did the Pinewood Derby, Cal and Ryan did quite well with Ryan taking first and Cal taking second in our pack. They were quite proud of themselves and Ryan being Ryan almost got himself a whooping after taunting Cal with the first place trophy.

As they progressed through the ranks I also advanced on the parent side, going from being an involved parent to Cub Master within a year. I skipped right past the whole den mother/father thing and even hurdled through assistant Cub Master when the guy who was going to train me abruptly quit, leaving me a box of files and errant papers to figure it out.

This was 2001 and 2002 so the internet wasn't the greatest yet but between the limited capabilities online and paper manuals, I was able to figure it all out and keep the program running on the right track. Based on the positive feedback, I know I did a pretty good job. However, I can remember one den mother who became a friend of mine looking me right in the eyes and saying "what you really need is a good woman who will help you take control of your life." As well as I thought I was doing I must have come off as a bit frazzled or even a little lost in life. That comment always stuck with me.

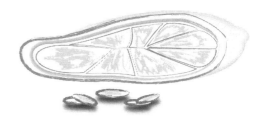

CHAPTER TWELVE
Finding My Pillar of Strength

*"You are the average of the five people
you spend the most time with."*

Jim Rohn, American Entrepreneur,
Author and Motivational Speaker

I believe in the power of the Law of Attraction.

During each segment of my life prior to getting divorced I surrounded myself with people who were most like me at the given time. This created and recreated the environment I was most accustomed to which can be summed up in one word — chaotic.

That all started to change before my divorce began in June of 2000 with the biggest change or "event" occurring shortly after the divorce was finalized in January of 2003. This "event" was meeting and then marrying Stacey, which I consider to be the same event that all rolls into one common occurrence that brought my life into focus, providing the solid spiritual, mental and emotional stability it had always lacked.

We met at Chuck E. Cheese's on a Friday night. I was still in my work clothes and originally had other plans to go to a bachelor party with some fraternity brothers. My ex-wife decided she wanted to go out, so she called me and said the kids are mine or she's getting a sitter. Of course I jumped at the chance to have the kids, so I changed plans and picked them up.

Soon after they got in the car, Cal reminded me that the last time we were together, which was last weekend, we attempted to go to Chuck E. Cheese's but never made it. So I had promised that the next time we're together we're going. My intent was the following weekend of regular visitation but being a dad of his word we went to the one in Geneva, Illinois.

Little did I know that while in line waiting to pay for our pizza and fun, the woman who was going to change my world forever walked in with her kids, and a friend's child, and was in line right behind us. I didn't notice her until I walked to the dining room after paying and, for whatever reason, turned the opposite way. I did a full circle and I almost walked into her face to face.

All I can remember is thinking to myself, "Whoa, now this is one heck of sweet physical specimen!" But, of course, I had to play it cool so I said, "Excuse me" and proceeded to the table with the kids without looking back, acting like it was no big deal or that there was any real interest piqued on my part. Always gotta play it cool — the guys will know what I mean here.

Now, Stacey and I both agree that this was all meant to be because little did we know, this was an integral part of each of our post-divorce processes. The biggest lesson found in divorce is that it showed me that you can break out of a horrible situation, put a problem or an issue behind you, and start with a brand-new and better situation, a predestined situation.

As the night progressed I would check her out once in a while and I would catch her checking me out too, but I never spoke to her — just couldn't bring myself to hit on a mom at Chuck E. Cheese's with her kids, it just didn't seem right. But boy was she, and still is, something good to look at!

I vividly remember the point where the ice was finally broken. My daughter had cut her finger and I was going to see if they had a bandage.

We were seated at the tables along the windows, my back to the dining/play areas, and as I turned Stacey was standing there waiting to talk to me. I was so shocked that when she asked if I wanted a beer I couldn't get the words out and answered with a "Huh?"

She says she instantly panicked thinking I'm a "Duh," like most of the other men she has had in her life. She quickly tried to talk some more so she could see if I was able to carry on a conversation like a normal human being — now that's some funny stuff!

She proceeded to ask if it was okay coming to talk to me and by now I was getting my wits about me. Finally able to speak coherently I said, "Yeah, it's okay," all the while the butterflies were going to town, I was nervous as heck — this absolutely beautiful woman was taking the initiative to talk with me!

We wound up closing the place down that night. We talked for hours, the kids all hung out and got to know each other — one of the biggest hurdles in a divorce situation that involves kids was resolved before we even got to know each other. I later learned the whole asking me if I wanted a beer was a ploy to meet me with a topic of conversation — she doesn't even drink, she just thought it would be easier to approach me that way, rather than come right up and start talking. I confessed how I just couldn't bring myself to hit on a mom at Chuck E. Cheese.

She added that the whole question about whether it was okay she was talking with me was because of the "Huh?" comment I made.

She saw no ring, still in work clothes on a Friday night and disheveled looking kids — all signs of a divorced dad, but the "Huh?" threw her off. I told her it was a "Huh?" out of complete shock I was being hit on by someone I thought could have never been single.

But, as fate would have it, we were both single and ready to travel down the road to a serious relationship. As a matter of fact I didn't even wait the statutory 48 hours to make the first call — I called her the first thing the next morning and the next phase of my life began.

Right from the beginning there was something about Stacey that just seemed so normal and calm. Think about it this way — by now you have a good feel for all the crap that comes along with me and then I meet the daughter of Ward and June Cleaver. Everyone in her immediate family hugs, kisses, says I love you, gets "angry" with each other when they're actually pissed, but nobody beats the hell out of anybody else.

"What do you mean you're angry with your sister? Kick her ass and ask questions later..." but they didn't and it was very different to me and, in the beginning of our relationship, almost odd.

However, in time I came to like it and slowly started to adopt their ways. At times, though, my inner core still puts on the brakes saying, "Whoa, this is all so foreign and unnatural and almost seemingly out of character for any human being to want to live this way."

At this point there is an internal struggle between good and evil, wherein my natural inborn instincts start rearing their ugly little heads and want to take over. I have come to the realization that I will always have to remain cognizant of this and correct myself before the engrained socially unacceptable behaviors take over.

Stacey provides a strong personality and is a person for me to lean on in hard times. She is strong and does not let things lead her astray from what is important, just like me. What is important to me now is completely different than what was important to me before I met Stacey.

Stacey's priorities have always been God, family, then work — mine have completely flipped from Tom, Tom, work, then a fine line between Tom again and family, work again, then God to now: God, family, work then me. I was so concerned about making sure I was number one and making as much money as fast as I could by working crazy long hours that I never even gained sight of the real important things in life in the first place.

But then again, I never had a family structure that was worth putting first before Stacey came along, and you already know my feelings on God and faith. The kids were always number one to me but the complete family structure was never there — how could it be when I never really rid myself of the cycle by marrying into what I wanted to put behind me?

It's amazing how this subtle change in priorities has changed me as a person. I missed out on so much in life by adopting the priorities determined by my environment from childhood, to when I met Stacey at age 36 in 2003. It wasn't a quick change, but rather gradual and continual with Stacey there to help guide me along the way.

The last bit of "oomph" I needed to complete the transformation came when Cal died and we started Cal's Angels. My new priorities were now set and I will never look back.

At the end of the day, it would be very difficult to continue without Stacey being there to take care of things. She is my rock. She does not crumble, fall or fail. She puts up with my ex-wife's antics and irrational, inexplicably bizarre behavior.

Because I work a lot, Stacey takes a great deal of responsibility for our kids. Don't get me wrong — while I work a lot at both of my jobs — the insurance gig and Cal's Angels, plus writing this book — I do take a lot of time off to spend with my family because I will never forget where they rank in my priorities. Stacey keeps telling everybody how this is the best relationship she has ever had and I have to say without hesitation that the feeling is mutual — we are the best of friends and we absolutely respect each other.

While we may not go to church all the time or carry a Bible with us, God is still and will always be number one on both of our lists. I thank Him every day for everything I have in my life and especially for sending me to Chuck E Cheese's that day in 2003.

CHAPTER TWELVE TAKEAWAYS — DISCUSSION TOPICS

- **Can changing your priorities change your life? If so, can it flow both ways — for the better and for the worse?**

- **Is the "Law of Attraction" real or just psychobabble?**

- **What are your thoughts on Jim Rohn's quote about being the average of the five people you spend the most time with? True? False?**

- **Are chance encounters like mine with Stacey at Chuck E. Cheese's really by chance or are they part of one's predetermined plan?**

CHAPTER THIRTEEN
Understanding the "Why" of it All

"Every adversity, every failure, every heartache carries with it the seed of an equal or greater benefit."

Napoleon Hill
American Author on Personal Success
(Think and Grow Rich, Outwitting the Devil)

B ack in my heyday I did everything I could so that no one would ever "get the best" of me and "win" in any situation. Whether it be taking off from the red light, gaining control of a lane of traffic, getting through the merge area first, arriving at the checkout lane before the other guy meandering through the aisles or pretty much anything else in life that could be considered a race or contest, I was going to give it my all to come out of it as the victor.

I'll bet half of these people who "challenged me" probably never even knew there was a contest going on. That is until I made a dick move to forcefully cut them off or do something else to irritate them then it was sometimes game on or they just quietly blended in with the background. I always felt it was at that point I won but little did I know it was the non-reactionary ones who actually won in the long run.

How did they win you ask?

Simple: they carried on with life in the same fashion they always have. Their car did not get wrecked, their nerves were not rattled, they weren't looking over their shoulder to make sure the guy they just pissed off isn't coming up for a blind side attack and they had the pleasure of allowing someone to have their way without harming their own sense of self-worth and dignity.

When I started looking at life differently and thinking about others first, I learned that you don't always need to be first to win. In certain situations, allowing others to have the physical win but capturing the mental and emotional win is much more fulfilling. Of course, there are certain things like when you're selling for a living taking anything but first makes it hard to put food on the table but in general just taking the high road in most situations makes life all that much more fulfilling. I no longer fight for the lane in traffic, race to the checkout lane, burn rubber from the stop light — if someone really wants something that petty that badly they can have it and I spend my energy on something else.

I could turn bitter in these situations but instead I turn better and will never have to look back over my shoulders again keeping my head focused on the path out in front of me where my bright future ripe with opportunity lies.

How I react to situations has changed and I'm never looking back.

Does everything happen for a reason?

Is there a hidden purpose or meaning for everything that happens?

Whether right or wrong, real or perceived, I try to tell myself that no matter what it is that has happened, there is a reason for it and through that comes acceptance of any given situation or circumstance.

I'm not saying that I'm happy with everything that occurs in my life and there are certain situations that I may not ever agree with. That said: When I can break things down as life lessons to learn from or use them for personal growth, it is then that I am able to get through whatever it is life throws at me.

For lack of better words, this is my coping mechanism. Even when the "why" is not obvious nor does it reveal itself at all, I still believe the reason will become clear at some point in my life.

In life in general I have found that people really only understand those who are — or have been at some point in time — near the same level of intellect, spirituality and socioeconomic status as they are themselves. I've found that I have a pretty good insight into most people because of my diverse background and wide range of life experiences including:

- being a child in an alcohol fueled environment subjected to physical and mental abuse

- going from the bullied to the bully of the bullies

- being a family of little net worth that evolved to an affluent family

- from a law-abiding citizen to being incarcerated back to law-abiding citizen

- going from being "husky" with buck teeth and Coke bottle glasses to jock

- going from jock to drug and alcohol user

- going from shy to outgoing salesman

- going from being forced to believe in God to steering clear of God to becoming a true believer in God

- going from married with children to divorced and married again with a set of his, hers and our children

- going from okay dad at best to dad who keeps trying to get better at it

- going from healthy family to pediatric cancer family who lost a child

- and, finally, going from only thinking about me to thinking about and living for the good of others

I know how most people on each level think, act and react under most circumstances.

After losing Cal, I took a real hard look at myself from the inside out and then back in again all the while searching for a reason why such a young life ended the way it did.

It took a few years and some reminders from lessons I've learned through the Cal's Angels organization, but I was able to realize that everything I've experienced in life (every trial and every tribulation) is part of a process that was training me for my real purpose in life — my true definite purpose for being here on this earth. Why did God put me here and what am I supposed to do with all I have experienced and all that I have at my fingertips? I'm supposed to help others before helping me, myself and I.

When you lose a child, it violates the natural order of things. Words do not come easily but emotions certainly do and everyone responds differently. What is consistent for everyone is that the world as they once knew it has changed forever ...

Hopefully somewhere along the line you find your way back again. That "back" will never be the same as you once knew it to be. Something has changed. Something has definitely changed and you know — you feel it in your inner soul — that you're somehow different.

That change can drive you into the ground; it can cause you to give up and flush it all down the toilet.

Or ...

... if you're sensitive to that change, it just might realign everything. It might bring you to a far better place and help you to either define your true definite purpose for the first time ever or redefine what you initially thought was your true definite purpose in life. In my case, I found that every trial and every tribulation is part of a process that was training me for my real purpose in life.

Out of respect for the feelings and privacy of others over the years since Cal passed, I have not shared much of anything with those going through similar situations unless first asked to do so. I know how they feel, how they act and what they think. The biggest reason I hesitate to bring it up first is because they are going through a very hard time and many are often in denial of just how serious the situation really is.

While I do not actively bring it up myself, I always leave it open for them to bring it up to me. I guess I do not always know my place in bringing things like this up — is my advice welcome? Are they uncomfortable bringing it up because they know my boy lost his battle with the same disease their child is fighting? Would they rather just suffer in silence as some think the less you talk about it the less serious it is?

Recently, though, things are different. To people who have not gone through it, I don't shy from the subject. I bring it up openly so that they know I'm okay with talking about everything I have experienced along this journey.

For those going through it at that particular time, I will tell them that I know what they are going through and I know how they feel. I stress that I have been there before and my family went through the same ordeal. I assure them that even though I wish I didn't know all of this, I've turned the experience into something helpful and I may as well be there to help others in any way I can help. I make sure to let them know it's okay if they want to be left alone. I just want them to feel comfortable talking with me about anything at any time whenever they want. I want them to know I am okay talking about anything I've gone through and communicate to them how this applies to anyone and any situation.

When they're ready or interested, they come talk with me. If it isn't me they talk with, it's my wife Stacey. She adds a whole new dimension to it all as stepmom and Mom. She's more than earned the title of a "real" mother to Cal, but she also bears the "stepmom" moniker and that provides her the ability to connect on more levels than just one.

People being people, the opposite sometimes happens too. There are those who will deliberately avoid bringing up the subject of losing a child (or even the subject of kids at all) around someone who has experienced such loss, or whose child is seriously ill.

I remember being at a golf outing and anytime the subject of kids would come up, one of the guys in our group would instantly change the subject. After finally catching on to what was happening, I told him that I was okay with talking about anything relating to Cal, family, kids, cancer and health. Turns out one of the other people at the outing had told him my story and he wouldn't even talk about his own kids because he thought it would be uncomfortable for me.

That having been said: some people who have been through something like this just cannot talk about it, so I tread very lightly. I don't ever want anyone to feel like a failure, or like they have "problems" because they have not yet come to terms with the situation like I have.

Everyone deals with things on different levels and at different speeds. Whether someone heals from these wounds quickly or takes years has no bearing on what kind of person they are. It's those who never heal that I feel the most need to help in any way I can. Actually, I don't think you can ever fully heal — I know I will never but it's what you do to carry on that makes the difference.

Sometimes I will tell people, "You know, we have seven children. Five live with us full-time, one lives with his mother most of the time and one lives with God."

I bring that up early in conversation so they know I am comfortable talking about it.

I always tell everyone that the only thing worse than losing your kid to any disease is in the case when the child dies suddenly and without warning. I had time to hang out with Cal and really get to know him through those one on one times in the hospital room. Yes, he was sick but we had some great bonding times. There are parents out there who lose a child suddenly and they never get to say that last goodbye. They never get to give that last hug or kiss knowing it is the last one. They think the last one will never come before they die and then it happens and they realize the last "quick peck on the cheek" or "half-hearted hug" was the last one forever. And God forbid they had a fight during their last moments together. While it's hard enough having lost Cal, I think any of these situations would have been worse. Still, they're all the same in the end: your child is gone and you have to somehow carry on without him or her or — even worse — them.

It is thoughts like these that really get to me at times and make me want to just give up. Sometimes I want to put my head through a wall, sometimes I just punch the wall or scream as loud as I can for as long as I can before ultimately breaking down in tears. Sometimes it's nothing more than a slight sob. Other times it's a full on bawling session complete with cursing and questioning God. Why Cal? Why did you have to take him?

Bob is an insurance client of mine who has become a good friend and confidant when it comes to faith. Bob is very into faith and the Book (and for those of less faith by "the Book," I mean the Bible.) He and I have had long conversations about faith, God, Jesus and predestination and how all of this fits into the master plan.

I said, "I lost my boy. However, there has to be some reason for this to have happened."

I told Bob how folks challenge me and ask, "You lost your son. How can you say there is a God if you lost your son?"

He agreed it is a great question and asked how I respond.

I told him how I see it in the grand scheme of things.

God sent his only son to be with us. He sacrificed his son to make things better for us. In no way am I comparing or saying Cal is Jesus, but if God can do this and still believe in us then how can I be upset with him or what has occurred with Cal? Cal was here for a purpose and a reason to be in my life to make me slow down and love while making an impact on everyone's life he touched not just while he was alive but long after he passed.

He did not pass slowly. It was long, protracted and filled with suffering, but also filled with promise.

Included here is a series of entries from the comprehensive diaries I kept during my time with Cal in the hospital:

May 8, 2006, 2:32 p.m.

After having reached a high of 147 Friday night, Cal's white cell count is down to 17 and still dropping, his spleen and liver are functioning fine and there does not seem to be any major concern with fluid around the heart. Despite all of this good news, he is experiencing severe pain, which keeps getting worse as the day goes on, in his lower right abdomen going around into his lower back - he is absolutely miserable. With all organs functioning correctly, the doctors are puzzled and are hoping the ultra sound scheduled for 4:00 p.m. today gives us some answers.

With regards to the transplant, the cord blood search is going very well. They have many initial matches and will be finished with the final DNA/ Chromosome testing sometime in the next week or so. Once the infections are cleared up and the pain has subsided, he should be ready to start the transplant process soon after testing is complete.

May 9, 2006, 8:47 p.m.

18 hours later and we still have no solid answers just suspicions as to what is causing Cal's pain which, at some points, was absolutely unbearable until they juiced him up with so many and such high doses of pain killers that he finally passed out at some point mid-morning. His white cell count has gone back up slightly, he was having trouble breathing so now he's on the full oxygen set up with the sealed mask and all, there is still some fluid around the heart and now some around his lungs, he spiked another fever over 102 indicating another infection and has not eaten in 48 hours. He's had 6 different sets of x-rays, a CT scan, countless blood and urine tests, an ultra sound, a Doppler ultrasound and numerous exams by specialists from several disciplines as well as the ICU team and the doctors are still baffled as to what is the root cause. Several possibilities include small kidney stones that can't be seen by the scans or x-rays, abdominal cavity infections, blockage in the bladder or one of several latent chemo or transplant related issues. Cal has endured something I would not even wish on my enemies but through it all he has hung tough, tougher than anyone else I know could have or even would have done.

May 10, 2006, 8:33 p.m.

The last few days cannot be described in words — there is just no way to get what Cal has gone through down on paper and have someone comprehend it.

On the bright side, Cal finally started feeling better this afternoon — well enough to have Wendy's Nuggets and a Frosty for dinner — his first real food since Sunday! He also spent an hour or so downloading songs and videos from iTunes for his iPod then watched some TV before passing out again from the pre-meds he received for his second blood and platelet transfusion of the day.

With regards to the cause of all this, they have narrowed it down to a few things which could have all occurred at the same time. One, the rapid breakdown of the white cells and blast cells when his counts dropped from 147 to 17 could have caused a toxic reaction in the kidneys, bladder and related areas - his white cell count has since leveled off below five. Another, in addition to the fluid around his heart and lungs, he has fluid in his lungs which is not pneumonia but could be an infection which they tested for today by sticking a camera through his nose and down into his lungs taking pictures and drawing out the fluid — the buildup of all this fluid could have put extreme downward pressure on all of his organs causing severe pain — let me tell you, Cal did not have a good time with this procedure as neither would anyone else — the doctor that performed the procedure said that Cal is the most cooperative patient he can remember, including the adult patients, which made his job easy. Lastly, they have not ruled out a general infection in the abdominal cavity which was undetectable on any of the scans and has not yet shown up in a blood culture.

At least things are looking up and we're looking forward to a much better day tomorrow. He's already off of the oxygen mask (he only has the two prongs in the nose) and hopefully he'll be off of the pain meds which are now less than half of what they were just this morning.

Cal is looking forward to several visitors from home tomorrow — first his grandma and aunt will be here in the morning then his mom is bringing his brother and sister — they're leaving right after school and will be staying overnight — I'm sure they're bummed about missing school on Friday. Sometime on Friday they'll be heading home with me while his mom stays until we switch off again at the end of next week.

(For those interested in reading more about Cal's journey in the hospital, visit http://caringbridge.org/visit/calsutter.)

I have no other choice but to believe that his life had a purpose. That purpose was to set all this up for what I have become and what I am doing today. Cal's life was part of a larger process, aiding me to figure out my purpose in life. His death was the final and most important phase of the process.

Without that, there would be no Cal's All-Star Angel Foundation. I would still be the person who thought only about himself. I would still be the person who forever thought he was on the fast track into heaven by donating a hundred bucks to people who ask me to support their cause.

There is a difference between trying to buy your way into heaven and earning your way into heaven. Living to help others first while absolutely enjoying doing so without any expectation of anything in return is a pretty good start.

CHAPTER THIRTEEN TAKEAWAYS — DISCUSSION TOPICS

- Does everything happen for a reason?

- Is there a hidden purpose or meaning for everything that happens?

- What are coping mechanisms you use to come to terms with things that are hard to explain? How about when the times get tough?

- Is it easy to understand people when they are not like you at all?

- Conversely, is it easy to understand them when they are just like you in every way?

- What is your "true definite purpose" in life?

- If you don't know, how will you find it?

- If you do know, how do you really know it is your "true definite purpose" in life?

CHAPTER FOURTEEN

Just a Random String of Coincidences? You be the Judge...

"The two most important days in your life are the day you were born and the day you find out why."

Mark Twain, aka Samuel Langhorne Clemens,
American Author and Humorist

It's easy to just sit back and let life happen without taking note of what is really going on around you. All too often people just assume that what is occurring or has happened is part of the normal routine... that is, until they take notice.

So when did I first become aware that the events in my life may be more than just a string of mere coincidences?

There are way too many impactful things that have happened in my life for me to believe that they occurred randomly without rhyme or reason. It hit me like a ton of bricks when I started attending a men's group that had formed in our neighborhood. A group of guys started it as a support group for me right after Cal passed away. The initial formation of the group is an interesting story.

A few months before Cal passed away, I was on the driveway putting a few things away in my car when one of the members of the as-yet-unformed group (a man whom I had never met before) pulled up and invited me to be part of the church softball team. In time I got to know some of the guys pretty well. After Cal passed away they invited me to join their men's group, passing it off like the group had been around for quite a while. In reality, the group had never even met yet. They were waiting for me to agree. I was reluctant, but yet at the same time willing to join. I later found out that it was formed specifically for me. They started the group because they did not want me to lose faith, give up hope or be bitter in any way, adding that they all wanted to be there for me to lean on for support in any way needed — spiritually, mentally, emotionally, financially or for anything else I or my family may have needed.

We started out with about six members meeting at Christ Community Church and had upwards of 11 of us at the peak height. Our meetings ran a little over an hour at six o'clock in the morning during the week and we eventually wound up at various members' homes along the way due to space constraints at the church.

All along Stacey thought it would be good for me to step out of my routine, get together with them and have some interests outside of work and family. She never tried to force me into the group, but was very supportive of it. Though she never gives me a direct answer of yes or no when I ask, I think she was in on this from the beginning.

Shortly after I joined the softball team and got involved with the men's group, Stacey joined a women's Bible study group in our neighborhood where she met a lot of women. Several of them are still close friends of hers.

I, on the other hand, have maintained casual contact with most of my group but don't have very close ties with any of them except for one (who is now more of a close acquaintance.) I know he and his wife would do anything for us in a heartbeat and we would do the same — we just so happen to run in different circles of close knit friends is all.

In the group we did a lot of reading and group studies on the Bible as well as books geared towards stimulating discussions within men's groups like ours. One of the books we read stands out the most and had the greatest impact on my thought processes as a whole: "The Case for the Creator." It talked about how even some of the greatest scientists find it difficult to dispute the argument that there are just too many coincidental things that have occurred in our world for it all to be chance and circumstance.

When you really take it all in and try to explain that everything just happened by chance you either stumble on your words or sound like you're making it up. These are a few things that continue to fascinate me every day:

- Birds — every different shape, size, color and sound each one makes

- Bugs — especially those pesky mosquitoes, what's the deal with them or even the earwigs, flies, gnats, cockroaches and on and on

- Plants, Trees, Flowers and Weeds — all varieties

- Rain, sleet, snow, wind, clouds, temperature, humidity, air pressure, jet streams, high tide-low tide, algae, seaweed, rocks, mountains and tundra

- Animals — way too many to even start

- People — men, women, race, religion, color, dialect, accent, believers, non-believers, moral, ethical or just plain evil

That's not everything but you get the point.

This was only a month or two after Cal had passed away and, based on what I read in the book, it became quite clear that there just has to be a creator, a master of all mankind — God is real and God does exist. If God exists then there has to be a heaven and if there is a heaven then I know that is where Cal resides.

From the day Cal died we saw "signs."

For instance, Cal had a magnetic dolphin in his room that, due to a metal weight that made it bottom heavy, just kept swinging pendulum style on a wheel of sorts. We got it from Dave & Buster's — one of his favorite places and one of the last ones we visited as a family for his birthday right before his diagnosis. Cal passed away at 10:05 p.m. on August 28, 2006.

We came home after the funeral a few days later and the weighted dolphin had stopped at what would be 10:50 p.m. on a dial faced clock. The weight defied gravity at that location and should be down at 10:30 p.m. Uncle Ray, who is a true believer, said it was obvious why it had stopped at 10:50 p.m.: It took Cal 45 minutes to get all checked in at heaven with 10:50 p.m. being the time he passed through the gates. He was letting us know he was all settled in, safe and sound. Out of curiosity, checking to see if it was a flaw in the manufacturing, I did eventually let the dolphin start swinging again and it never stopped in a gravity defying position again.

On the day he passed, my youngest sister was driving up from the University of Illinois to say goodbye to Cal. She was driving my grandfather's car — the infamous "Pop" (if you recall from my earlier stories), and the coolest grandfather in the world who loved everyone (especially his grandkids and great grandkids). He was a true giver and a strong believer in God.

My sister proceeded to tell me that as she's driving the car it stalled on the highway — not even at a light or parked, but on the highway while she was driving 60 around 10:10 p.m. No rhyme or reason. It just stalled. My sister calls my parents who, in turn, called the highway car service. They arrived at around 11:00 p.m. and the car started right up with no issues even though she kept trying all along. It was as if Pop had been guarding the car but left to help make sure Cal made it to heaven safely and then went back to the car after he checked in.

In the same vein, ever since I can remember Cal had the number 9 on his jersey. At first, he didn't go into it saying he wanted number 9, but rather it was assigned to him based on how his height fit in with the rest of his team. Shortest got number 1 and they cycled through the numbers until they got to Cal. He was given the number 9. From then on, it became his number and he always requested it for his jersey.

After Cal passed, South Elgin Little League retired his number across all teams for a year and let only his siblings have it on their jerseys. They also purchased special baseballs and softballs with the number 9 sporting a halo on them.

As a lifelong tribute to Cal and our family, the park district allowed them to rename the last field he played on at Jim Hansen Park (formerly Concord Park) the "Cal Sutter Field" and included the number 9 with a halo on the sign.

I know number 9's are everywhere but there are those key moments when I need a boost or even just a reminder that Cal is looking down on us and smiling. It is in these times when I see a number 9 standing out from the norm. Perhaps on a door (as in door #9), or on a license plate that has only the number 9 on it. Maybe on a pro athlete's jersey on TV, or I might find that I only have $9.00 left in my wallet, etc. You get the picture: The number 9 carries a lot of meaning for us.

Another time that sticks out is when we went to the same Dave and Buster's where Cal won the dolphin. We had all the kids with us. Everyone wanted to play some games so the kids scattered about.

Jessie headed for a game where you win tickets based on your timing. By hitting a button, you earned more points depending on where you stopped the line of lights going up the pole. As we rounded the corner, Jessie was just standing there looking up at the area that normally lists the number of tickets in the jackpot. Rather than numbers it said "Cal." Nothing else was working on the game.

As we were all standing there looking up at the machine in a state of shock, one of the staff members came over and opened the machine's front door panel. He handed Jessie a wad of tickets, congratulated her and apologized for the machine jamming. He flipped the "call" switch off and left. The number of tickets in the jackpot was returned to the appropriate box and the game was working correctly — what in the heck just happened?!

Jessie proceeded to tell us she never even put in a token or swiped her card — she turned the corner and saw "Cal" up top and was confused. From what I can tell someone before her won but it got jammed so they hit the call button, got tired of waiting and left. Jessie happened upon the situation at that moment and as the "call" appeared — the spot for the last "L" was either burned out or only three letters showed up. Either way, the odds of this all actually occurring like it did seemed extremely high.

Then there was the time we were on spring break in Florida.

We went into the combination ice cream-pizza parlor at the resort where there was a guy playing an acoustic guitar and singing songs from the 1970's. You know what I'm talking about: Eagles, Clapton, Journey, Rick Springfield… and then, all of a sudden, he throws in "Good Riddance" by Green Day in the middle of it all.

We all looked at each other with shock and awe on our faces while the goose bumps were making their presence felt. "Good Riddance" is one of the songs Cal put on a CD for me before he died. At the time I didn't know he even knew who Green Day was, yet here is their song on this CD alongside other tracks like "Had a Bad Day" by Daniel Powder (plus some Beastie Boys, among others.)

One time I was driving the back country roads through farmland on a sunny afternoon during the week and Good Riddance came on the radio. This feeling of extreme sadness mixed with anger came over me and consumed my inner soul. My foot pushed the pedal to the floor while I grabbed the steering wheel so tight and pulled as hard as I could. I thought I was going to rip it right off of the steering column. When I finally looked down I was going 140 and still climbing. Then it hit me — what the heck am I doing? I'm no good to anyone dead! How selfish and ignorant am I? If I die who takes care of my wife? My kids? My teams at both businesses? The Cal's Angels recipient families? I took my foot off the gas and gently applied the brakes to slow down to the speed limit of 55. Luckily, I had just been on a flat, straight road through open farm country and my car was able to handle the outburst.

By putting Good Riddance as the first track on the CD I truly believe there was some foreshadowing of events and advice to live by — here is the first full verse and chorus; you be the judge.

Another turning point, a fork stuck in the road

Time grabs you by the wrist, directs you where to go

so make the best of this test and don't ask why

it's not a question, but a lesson learned in time.

It's something unpredictable but in the end is right

I hope you had the time of your life.

There are several interpretations one can gather from the song and, even though we never told him his life was nearing its end, Cal knew the song would be here forever. As I break it down in an effort to understand the purpose of it all I now know there's a whole message I believe Cal was trying to get across to me.

His death would be a huge turning point — the proverbial fork stuck in the road. When faced with a similar situation, it is at this point you can turn bitter by giving up and flushing your life down the toilet or better by turning what is the worst possible negative into a positive force.

It is an adversity so strong that the negative part of it can bring you down further than anything else if you let it. On the flipside, however, it is so strong that the positive part of it can catapult you to new heights you've only dreamed of if you are aware and conscious enough of the hidden opportunities.

You sometimes have no direction to follow, no path so you have to throw it up in the air and put it in His hands to guide you.

This is a test of your sanity, your wits and you as a person in general. Make the best of what you are dealt and don't ask why — it is what it is and there's nothing you can do about it so do your best with what life has dealt you.

There is no way to predict something like this and as wrong or unnatural as it is to have a parent bury their child, in some strange way it was supposed to be this way. It may not really be "right" but it is the way it was supposed to be — the purpose behind Cal's time on this earth.

The last line is Cal's way of saying to live life like he did — have fun, don't take everything seriously and always have the time of your life.

An alternate "all in one" summary of the entire song is that the death of a child or any other similar "shock to the system" is a turning point in one's life — you have two choices in most situations and the path you take is not always clear at first. You sometimes have to make up your mind to do what you think is right and go for it. Make the best of it without asking why for there is no question to be asked, just a lesson to be learned. It somehow seems like it was supposed to be this way.

This interpretation of the song comes into play when talking about what we did and what we were thinking when we established Cal's All-Star Angel Foundation. After Cal's death we realistically had only two choices — give up and stick our heads in the sand or turn a horrible negative into an extremely positive force by creating an entirely new 501(c)3 not-for-profit organization modeled after the way Cal lead his life — thinking about others before himself.

We never really asked why but rather just did it and figured the answer to all of this would eventually come. The success we have achieved is both completely gratifying and reveals the answer as to why Cal was put here in our lives and ultimately suffered. It is now all so clear that the purpose of Cal's short, but meaningful, life was to teach every one of us — especially me — that it is much more gratifying to help others and think about others before ourselves.

I'll never say it's right but it was supposed to happen this way as I know I never would have done any of it if he would have survived or ever been diagnosed in the first place. We never saw it coming but now that we know it, have lived it and still live it we go to the extreme to continue to do it very well and enjoy doing it.

Of course, we'd give it all up to have Cal back. Unfortunately, that won't happen, so here we go: Seven years in and we're only just beginning our journey down this new path in life. We always do our best and always make sure we are having fun while enjoying every step along the way.

In his last days Cal knew he was dying even though we never told him. The Friday afternoon before he passed he called his mom and me to his bedside — I can remember it vividly, something that is etched into my memory forever with me on his left side and his mom on his right side.

As we were looking down at him he proceeded to tell us he wanted to be cremated. It seemed like the world stopped at that moment. While I had known he was dying all along, it was now clear that he knew it, too, and it suddenly seemed so much more real than it had before. I remember that as soon as the words came out of his mouth I was overtaken by extreme sadness. I knew Cal's battle and suffering were over. My firstborn child — the big brother, the great athlete, the good kid and the true friend — was dying.

Cal gave his mom and me specific instructions for his ashes. We were to split them 50\50. He told his mom that he wants her to save her half for when she dies. He wanted to have his ashes mixed with hers and thrown over the Grand Canyon — she always told the kids that's what she wants with her ashes so Cal wanted to be a part of it.

Cal looked at me and said, "Dad, with your half I want you to put some on the pitcher's mound in South Elgin, some on the mound at Cellular Field in Chicago, some in that lake in Canada we always talked about going to and save the rest for whatever it is you want to do when you die."

Then he told both of us, "Whatever happens, just don't let it turn out like that scene in Meet the Fockers where the urn falls off the shelf, breaks open and the cat pees on grandma's ashes."

Talk about a whole bunch of mixed emotions going on at once. First, it was so hard to wrap my head around the fact that I'm even having this conversation with my child. At the same time, Cal being Cal, he still had some lighthearted humor in him even in the toughest and darkest of times.

Second, I knew I could handle wishes one, three and especially four (by never letting any animals use his ashes like a litter box), but the whole Cellular Field thing was going to be difficult. So as I responded to him affirming all will be done, I couldn't help but picture myself having to jump over the wall during a White Sox game, rush the mound and throw ashes all the while security is chasing me, possibly thinking its anthrax that I'm dishing out, not ashes. Think back — right around 2005 and 2006, the big anthrax scares were popping up. It was a legitimate concern.

Putting some of his ashes on the pitcher's mound in South Elgin was simple and had a lot of meaning.

I went out there one night a little past midnight and spread his ashes around the pitcher's mound, mixing them into the dirt for good measure. Same as I did that night, I stop out there every once in a while and talk with Cal — I believe he can hear me, but whether he does or not doesn't really matter. Just doing it is great mental therapy.

Another cool story about that ball field is that I was the head coach of the White Sox playing on that spot for the first full year of it being called the "Cal Sutter Field." Cal's brother Ryan was on the team with his best friend and a couple other boys who would round out the team for several years to come.

We went through the entire season with one loss to the Rays. They also had one loss to us, so there we were at a one game playoff against the Rays to see who was going to move on to the Hamm's Tournament. The Hamm's Tournament is one step along the path in going to Cooperstown for the Little League World Series. They batted first and after the first inning and a half we were down 2 to 1.

It was at that point that Ryan came up to me and asked if I asked Cal for help. I told him that while I don't think Cal can actually help he knows people who can and that is what I asked him to do — ask everyone he knows up there to help us. That seemed to give Ryan some confidence as well as the rest of the team because the wheels fell off and we ended up with 17 runs by the fifth inning and added 10 more the next inning. That is where it ended in a slaughter rule 27 to 2 and we went on to the Hamm's.

The coolest photo I have is from after that fateful game with all the players and coaches hanging around the scoreboard where it says "Cal Sutter Field" holding up the number one sign on their hands — the bummer is that the parents from the other team demanded that the scoreboard be turned off so that their kids wouldn't be embarrassed, would have been nice to see that score in lights behind us. There was an angel in the outfield that day and his name is Cal: Always our angel and an angel of inspiration for all the kids and families we help.

The second of Cal's wishes of having his ashes on the pitcher's mound at Cellular Field was up next.

I put a call in to the head of public relations for the White Sox who said they have never received a request for this — ashes in the outfield, yes, but not on the pitcher's mound. She said she would have to get back to me. Two weeks later she called and said it went all the way up the chain to Mr. Reinsdorf who agreed to grant Cal's wish once the season was over!

The White Sox organization was very specific — no press, no flair and no more than six people — problem is we had five kids at the time plus Stacey and me (Ellie was not yet born.) Fortunately, they made an exception for us plus an additional person to say a prayer before spreading his ashes. The "additional person to say a prayer" was someone I always felt was a good friend, especially since he was one of the originators of the men's group for me.

One strange part about this White Sox wish is that my relationship with my parents spiraled downward and has never recovered. My mom wanted to attend the event so I told her about the rules set by the White Sox. She was having nothing of it and said she was going — that she'll call certain people she knows and get them to arrange for the White Sox to change the rules.

I said no and told her rules are rules so it's just our immediate family — it was quite an honor to have this privilege and I asked her to please not ruin it by making any calls. She proceeded to tell me how she's more family to Cal than Stacey and her kids — they should stay behind, not her. I told her that is so wrong and that she's not going — in my eyes, Stacey was more of a mom to Cal than even his own mom so the conversation is over.

I tried explaining that if I let her go then I would have to invite everybody: Dad, my two sisters, brother, his kids and wife, my aunts, etc. — she interrupted by saying none of them have to go, just her. I was really getting upset with all this, but at the same time I wasn't completely shocked. I decided to just do it without telling her in order to avoid confrontation. Little did I know avoiding the confrontation up front would alter the course of the rest of my life.

After we went I decided to tell her we did and she went off on me before hanging up. About a day or two later my dad called and told me I was the most despicable person he has ever met — he was shocked that I had cut them out of this event, especially my mom. It's crazy how rules don't seem to apply to them but that's how my mom has always been. In all reality, it's also how I behaved more often than not. It's a big reality check to see how you behave firsthand and realize why it is you behave that way — I knew deep down I had to change because it sure isn't a pretty sight to see nor is it anything pleasant for others to experience.

I am the classic case of matching and mirroring the parental behaviors I have been around all my life but never realized it until this played out. It takes a lot of work to get a lifetime of behavior modeling out of your system. It was going to take some real effort but I never want my kids to think about me and have the same realization I had about my own parents.

Needless to say, my relationship with my parents has never been the same and they still blame me for all of it.

From speaking with counselors they all say that they would have been shocked to hear that the relationship with my parents was still the same or that it even existed at all. It would show that I have not moved on and am still stuck in the past not realizing how wrong that sort of behavior and any other past behaviors really are.

Anyway, back to the story on the day we spread his ashes.

It was late afternoon at Cellular Field — greyish skies, cold and very still. We showed up at the corporate offices dressed for winter weather with his ashes and helium balloons to commemorate the event. A guy named Dane took us through the underground tunnel and up to the seats behind home plate. He opened the gates and let us onto the field. He told us to take all the time we wanted and then he left.

I had never been on a major league field before — talk about intimidating. I couldn't imagine the place being packed with the crowd looking down on you yelling and screaming. As I got to the pitcher's mound and looked all around in a 360° turn, I could almost feel the anxiety of the visiting pitcher or even the home pitcher when he messes up. There is nowhere to hide and the crowd is yelling whatever it is they want to yell at you.

As the rest of the gang joined me on the mound, reality hit and everything seemed so quiet again — the cold, still air, the grey sky and the completely empty ballpark except for us: Stacey, Ryan, Jessie, Jason, Kiley, Lexie and me. We were joined by our friend (as well as his wife, too) who said a few prayers before we each spread a spoonful of Cal's ashes on the mound and in the grass for good measure in case they ever tore up the mound. We released the balloons and took a lot of photos including each of us on the mound — these were good times that lasted for a couple hours before we sadly had to leave. We had dinner at Ed Dbevic's, another one of Cal's favorites, and then we headed home.

As of present I still have not made it up to the lake in Canada — Red Lake, Ontario, to be exact. The summer after freshman year of high school the wrestling coach and a group of dads brought 16 or so of us from Conant High School up there and we stayed at the Black Bear Lodge.

This is one of my ten all-time greatest memories — no electricity, running water or phones. Cut off from society and loving every minute of fishing — caught so many fish that were so big it's hard to describe. I still can't figure out how they grow so much bigger up north where the lakes are frozen over for much longer periods of time than in the Midwest.

From the day I got home from that trip up north I have always wanted to go back. I subsequently told Cal and Ryan that when Cal is 14 and Ryan is 12 we're going for the week long trip — they had always looked forward to it … obviously, based on Cal's request to bring his ashes up there, a lot more than I thought. This is still on my list and I will get there — the holdup is Ryan who says it sounded fun with Cal but way too scary without him. Now that he's older I'm sure he will go soon but in the interim we recently found a second-best option.

Ever since she was a kid, Stacey and her family went to a resort just outside of Park Rapids, Minnesota, called Brookside Resort. She got all of us to go for the first time the year after Cal passed away. Let me tell you, it is a great place for family time — no phones or TVs in the cabins but there is electricity and running water — cell service is spotty at best.

It takes a few days to untether from the world and get used to just relaxing but once you do, boy oh boy, the fun begins. They have a nine-hole golf course, tennis, an indoor and outdoor pool, sailing, mini golf, an old-fashioned snack shop complete with old fashioned scooped ice cream, hand dipped shakes, game room, fishing, tubing, waterskiing, games and more fishing. Funny how I don't go fishing all year but do it every day up at Brookside — maybe it's a prelude to what I'll be doing when I retire or what I would really rather be doing than work.

Along with our cabin by the lake we get our own fishing boat with a 5-horsepower outboard motor. We also rent our own ski boat for the week. It's very family-oriented and "north woodsy" — it's not rural and completely cut off like Canada but it's something I know Cal would have loved as much as the other kids do (including Ryan, who turned 19 before this year's trip.) As an indication of how great the trip to Brookside is, Ryan always looks forward to leaving his friends and job behind to join us for the full ten days we're gone.

Two trips ago — summer of 2012 — Stacey and I were talking about how I still hadn't made it to Canada to deliver Cal's ashes to the lake when she posed the question, "Do you think Cal would want to be up here in the lake at Brookside?" I didn't know the answer to that so I pondered it for a day or two. Still, I could not decide until a sequence of events led me to ask Cal.

One of the group's favorite activities at the resort is Bingo Night. This takes place on two separate evenings, the second one being on Thursday. While bingo is fun, I seize the opportunity for some of that oddly named "me time" and go fishing by myself.

That July Thursday in 2012 was a very clear, warm and still evening. The sun doesn't set until 9:30 p.m. or so that far up north and there are more stars filling the sky than you can imagine. There's at least one shooting star every evening — it's the stuff dreams are made of and it almost looks fake.

I remember it perfectly — there I am sitting out in the middle of the lake just after sunset in our ski boat, lights out and reeling in my lines. The loons are doing their eerie cries off in the distance, an occasional fish would jump and I could faintly hear the quiet chatter of the bingo game played out by the nearby pool as it was winding down.

It was at that perfect moment I sat down on the back of the boat, looked up at the unbelievable amount of stars and said out loud: "Cal, I know you heard us talking about bringing your ashes up to Brookside and you know I've toiled over the answer so please give me a sign if you want us to bring your ashes with us on the next trip up here in 2013."

I then finished packing up my gear, pulled up anchor and slowly motored in under cover of what was now a pitch black night except for the orange glow of the lights from the cabins off in the distance. I didn't tell anyone what I did as I wanted it to play out on its own.

The next morning I did my early-morning solo run on the lake and caught a few Northern Pikes on my Rapala Clackin' Raps — a decent outing but no sign from Cal. After breakfast we went to the favorite event of the last full day at the resort: The minnow races. It was a lot of fun for the whole family and it was during the distribution of the minnows that I got my sign.

The minnows race in these 20-foot long rain gutters filled with water. At one end there is usually one of the workers scooping a minnow into each participant's cup. The young man handing out minnows that day was sitting there wearing the scripted Cal hat: University of California — California Golden Bears.

I did a double take and was like Santa Claus checking his list twice — is this the sign I asked for or is he a college student (like most of the employees here) that just so happens to attend Cal? Curious minds like to know so I had to ask. If he did not go to Cal, why was he wearing that hat?

He told me he is not a college student at all and has at least 40 hats in his closet — this is the hat that jumped out at him today. Whoa! Is all I could think, this is the sign for sure. I told Stacey the story and she got goose bumps — Cal wants us to add Brookside as another final destination for a portion of his ashes and that's just what we did. Our 2013 trip included an "ashes in the lake" ceremony where each of us gently placed a little bit of Cal into Two Inlets Lake where he will forever be with us on our annual family vacations.

Things like this just keep continuing to happen and Cal's Angels continues to grow and flourish. It's pretty crazy for a couple of people like Stacey and I, outsiders to the charity world, starting a charity of our own.

Stacey has done a fair amount of volunteering and was raised in a charitable household but never ran a charity. It was a little different in my case as I'd never done much charity or nonprofit work, nor was I raised to be charitable. It all started with me having to figure out how to obtain the coveted 501(c)(3) designation on my own. This came after our initial group of 30 friends and neighbors helped us raise $73,000 after expenses at our first golf outing back in June of 2007.

When I look back now, my whole life has been a series of events and circumstances that set my life up to be this way: to do what I am doing with Cal's Angels. These "life events and circumstances," comprised of growing up the way I did, of all the craziness, all the chaos, the marital strife, my career choices, my difficult first marriage, my extremely expensive and mentally painful divorce to the subsequent costly and emotionally taxing custody battles, meeting and marrying Stacey, finding my way back to God and church, Cal's diagnosis, his battle and ultimate passing, and putting it all — including my life — in His hands and asking Him to do with it what He wants.

When you really boil it all down to the core, what do you think about all of it? What do you think about chance and circumstance or fate and predestination?

I'm going to answer my own question here: There was a definite master plan all along and it took a tragedy to make me realize it. Cal was put here in my life for one major purpose: To wake his old man up and force him to realize that he has the capacity and ability to do great things to help others.

I really don't like to brag, but if you have a spare 20 minutes to go to calsangels.org and see all that we have accomplished in seven years … tell me that's not the work of someone much higher-up than me. I guess I would also have to say that knowing it was supposed to be this way does make dealing with Cal's death a little easier. To know he did not die in vain is comforting in a way.

A friend of mine and someone I have introduced you to earlier in the book is John Davis. He's a strong believer with great faith, he loves his family, adores his wife Taksina, works hard and prays even harder. He asked me a question that didn't take me long to answer — the answer will always come quickly. He asked me, "Would you ever be doing any of this if it hadn't been for Cal and Cal's death?"

That answer was, is and always will be an emphatic, "Hell no!"

Why would it be a yes?

Prior to all of this I did a fair amount of thinking about myself first. I already mentioned my messed up priorities were: Tom, Tom, work, either Tom again or family, with everything else later on the list. Why would I spend my time helping others, especially when I can still hear my dad asking why he would give any of his hard earned money to people that do nothing for him? That was his philosophy, and it was mine by osmosis until we went through that ordeal with Cal. After those events my eyes were forever opened to the realities of the pediatric cancer world.

That's what I grew up thinking and believing — it's crazy how a tragedy opens your eyes. It feels so good to help others with no expectation of anything in return. I missed out on so much of the charitable aspects of life growing up. People like the person I had been for most of my life really need to try it. They need to mean it when they try it. They can't just do it because it makes them look good or because they think they can buy their way into heaven. It is absolutely fulfilling. It is exhilarating for the mind, body and soul.

You've already been introduced to my friend Bob. He is just like John when it comes to faith, family and life. Bob likened my life, and especially Cal's passing, to a play he saw in which Jesus was a potter. He starts out with just a plain lump of clay, then forms the base, or footing, which is you in your rawest form.

However, it is not centered. It's a little wobbly and crooked. As the pottery wheel spins his hands go around the clay in a loving way and it slowly becomes centered, perpendicular and well-balanced. The hand of God reaches inside and molds the pot — which is each one of us — from the inside out. It is your heart and soul. However, just like this shaped chunk of clay is not yet a finished product when it comes off the wheel, you are still not a perfect human being until you go through the fire and get the end product.

Bob said, "When I think of the play and all facets of it, I think of you and all the stuff you've gone through. All of this with Cal ... that was your journey through the fire. You came out on the other end as a completely new and different person but, most importantly, as a believer.

There is a higher purpose here for you and I know that you know it. I have told you for quite a while that you just needed to give it up and put it in His hands. You have lived through so many things and been through so much. You have so much in you to help others, but you need to let Him guide you. He will provide if it was meant for Him to provide — this will succeed if it was meant to succeed when it is placed in His hands to do with it what is supposed to be done.

You can only do so much to push it along, to force it to happen — the final stages are up to Him. You cannot change what is supposed to be. You can only alter its course for a moment. The end result will still be what was always meant to be."

He continued, "One of the first things you were meant to do is help people bring faith back into their lives. Show them that even in the worst of times, when it's easiest to give up on your faith, that faith itself is what helps you through anything. People are getting so far away from God. They're trying to push God out of the schools and their lives.

These people are losing faith, hope and belief. The more they lose it and distance themselves from God, the more apparent the results of doing so are. Just look around you, read the newspaper, watch the news — the evidence of what happens when you take God out of your life is all around you."

What Bob said rang so true and made me realize a lot of things I never really realized before ... but they were now becoming much clearer. I honestly believe that part of what I am here to do is to get people to believe again and have faith — give them hope that they can make it through life's trials and tribulations.

So many people just throw their lives away after they go through something like what we've gone through with Cal. There is nothing worse than losing a child and I am proof that life is not over when this happens but rather a new one is just beginning.

When Cal passed away it was an extreme shock to my system. The reason it was so extreme is because it lasted 14 ½ months from date of diagnosis to the day he died. I'm guessing that knowing my personality, it had to be a drawn out ordeal for me to experience and absorb the abnormalities of the whole situation. Like the clay vessel going through the fire and coming out on the other end a completely finished molded product, so too am I after Cal's battle and ultimate passing. It was a long slow process that carefully changed the molecular structure and makeup of the raw form, all resulting in a finished product with its own definite purpose for existing. This purpose was entirely redefined, or maybe even defined for the very first time ever.

I would say that by far the single most significant event in my life was going through this whole ordeal with Cal before ultimately losing him to cancer. It has forever changed who I am from my core, in and out. I now realize my entire life was setting me up to persevere through this event and beyond. This single, drawn out chapter of my life was meant to make me realize why I was born in the first place.

CHAPTER FOURTEEN TAKEAWAYS — DISCUSSION TOPICS

WHY THINGS HAPPEN:

- Do you ever find yourself assuming everything that happens in your life is all part of the normal routine?

- Do you believe your life is all part of a scripted plan to a predetermined end result?

WHO'S IN CHARGE?

- Do you believe in a Supreme Being or influencer like God, Mohammed, Buddha or another? Who do you believe in and why? If you do not believe, why not?

- Can you logically explain how everything came to be? Try just one of the topics I listed and explain it so everyone can understand it.

- Compare and contrast creationism vs. evolution. Which do you believe in? What's your argument to defend why you believe in that particular version of how everything came to be?

- Do you believe that loved ones who have passed send us "signs" in an effort to communicate?

COPING:

- What is your "going through the fire" life experience?

- When tragedy strikes, do you only have two choices or, in your opinion, are there more than two? If so, what are they?

- How has it changed you as a person?

- Is there a silver lining to most things that don't initially seem like they are good, right or proper?

WHY?

- Have you discovered your true definite purpose in life? If so, what is it? How did you discover it?

- Why were you born?

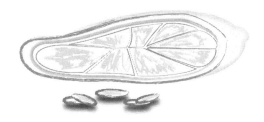

CHAPTER FIFTEEN
Faith and Purpose

"You can't reason with faith. That's why it's called faith:
It's not based on reason. It's the difference between
believing something to be true despite a lack of evidence
and thinking that something is true on the basis
of what evidence we have."

Huffington Post

I am very comfortable in talking about my faith, religion and spirituality. But just like my stance on politics, the one thing I will not do is debate anyone on either of these points. I will discuss it as long as you want but the conversation ends when the debate on any of it begins.

There are way too many friendships that have ended, more than enough relationships that have gone south and a socially unacceptable amount of physical altercations that have occurred for debating the differences in opinion to be worth anyone's while. I do not and will not force my opinions and beliefs on anyone. Everyone is free to believe what they want to believe. I know what I believe and that is all I need in order to be fulfilled.

While there is never really going to be a logical explanation for Cal's passing, I can tell you that through it all, and what has occurred since, my true definite purpose in life has become crystal clear. For example, my insurance business has continued to grow even when Cal was undergoing treatment for those fourteen and a half months.

Now, I am in a leadership role recruiting and training commercial insurance producers all the while growing my own book of business which has increased by 10% or more on a year over year basis. The producers who follow a proven program are generally "on track" and for whatever reasons, good, bad or indifferent, you will always have those who are charting an alternate course. I do not believe in the saying, "You can't teach an old dog new tricks."

While I was younger we had a black Labrador who continued to learn new tricks until he died at age 12 or so. While it's not the same comparison as to a person, it does prove that you can teach an old dog new tricks if he wants to learn new tricks. In one of the workshops I attended I heard the presenter add an interesting twist to the saying, "You can't teach an old dog new tricks, but you can't teach a stupid dog old tricks either."

I love leading and coaching — it started with training pledges in the fraternity and continued with coaching my kids' baseball and softball teams. The majority of these teams made it to the playoffs and several have even won championships during their first year together as a team. It has continued into business — a strong passion I have discovered within myself is guiding individuals to be successful in the first place, or more successful than they already are, by helping them to utilize their God-given talents.

Of course, this passion did not present itself willingly and only came into being after I was able to get past the "me first" persona that controlled my first 30 some odd years on this earth and discover the real reason why God placed me here and why he put me through some of the most trying trials and tribulations one can imagine.

While I may not be the highest producing commercial insurance guy around, I am at the high end of the middle bracket with well over a half million dollars in gross commissions and aiming to hit the three quarters of a million dollar mark here soon.

Pretty good but even more so intriguing when taking into account that at the same time I am building my own book of commercial insurance clients, I am also recruiting and training insurance producers while running a non-profit organization that has catapulted into one of the best around plus writing this book and being a good husband and father to six children.

Some may say I am boasting and bragging — almost looking for a pat on the back. It couldn't be more to the contrary. I know all of this is not my doing nor did it occur by chance — there is more involved here — a higher power guiding me in everything I do, every decision, every turn at every corner.

I used to have a strong desire to run my own insurance agency but that would bog me down and take me away from my core definite purpose in life. Do I need to own at least part of one or have a certain level of control to do it the way I feel is best and run it in the same fashion as I run Cal's Angels — that's a definite yes!

There are a lot of people in my life who have been there for me all of whom I want to take with me on this ride into the next phase of my life as it unfolds through the application of my definiteness of purpose. Question is, "Who will join me?"

Towards the end of Cal's fight with cancer, my sister traveled to the Vatican, purchased a crucifix, had it blessed by the Pope and gave it to Cal. He kept that crucifix either with him in his bed and/or at his bedside up there in Minnesota until the day we brought him home to live out his last days in his own bed. Good thing I know I'm forgetful, otherwise we might have left that crucifix behind at the University of Minnesota Hospital.

When the medical transport team came and moved Cal from the hospital bed onto the transport bed, they left the packing of Cal's items up to us. Cal's mom went with Cal and the transport team down the elevator to the ambulance while my family and I stayed behind to pack everything up. Thinking we had it all, we headed down the hall but something made me stop. For some reason I decided to head back to the room to give it a once over. If I weren't aware of my occasional forgetfulness, I may have brushed off this urge as a waste of time.

When I walked into the room, a nurse was in the process of taking the sheets off the bed, giving it a flick with her wrists. As the sheets unfolded towards the middle of the room I saw something fly out and I could hear a lighter in weight metal object hit the floor with a tinging sound. I looked down and there was the crucifix, lying Jesus side up as if he was saying "Don't forget me." I quickly snatched it up, threw it in the front pocket of my shorts with a feeling of relief that I had gone back, for if I hadn't, this sacred crucifix would have been gone forever.

As I exited the room, I can remember pausing and feeling a deep sadness like I was leaving home for good. Cal's mom and I had been switching off a week at a time for over three months, so while the hospital wasn't home, it was my home away from home. It represented the last place Cal was in remission and normal, or as normal as a kid who was fighting cancer could be. We were now headed to our real homes to spend what would be Cal's last few days on this earth. While I knew it was inevitable, part of me wanted to stay behind thinking if I did he would never be able to go home to die. I hesitated for a bit, but then in almost a robotic, self-programmed motion I headed down the hall, then the elevator and into the ambulance.

The ambulance drove us to the private medical transport jet where they loaded up Cal, hooked him to the machines and we were whisked to the St. Charles Municipal Airport by our house. The crucifix was in my pocket the whole time and when we finally got situated and Cal was in his own bed at his mom's house, I put the crucifix in his hand for him to touch it. I told him the story of how the crucifix made it and that it will be with him in his bed. While he didn't acknowledge hearing me, I know he did and it stayed in his bed under the sheets until he passed. Before it made its way elsewhere, I tucked it back into my shorts and vowed to never let it leave my possession.

I still have it to this day, eight years later, with only two major heart stoppers with it.

The first was when I had it in the front pocket of my jeans. We went to the hot dog place in town for lunch on a Saturday afternoon and the place was packed. There were at least 30 folks in front of us in a line that resembled the back and forth zig zag lines for the rides at Great America. As we got closer there were people coming in behind us. When I say it was packed, I mean it was shoulder to shoulder to get the food. This was in a shopping mall so no drive thru — thankfully most people were leaving rather than grabbing tables.

After paying, I was standing there waiting for the food when up comes this little boy from the middle of the crowd holding out his hand as he approached me. I looked down and in his hand was a crucifix. As I started to reach into my pocket to see if it was there he said "Sir, I think this is yours." When I came up empty handed I reached out and he gave it to me while I was sporting a look of complete shock on my face.

I looked at the crucifix, instantly knew it was Cal's and asked him how he knew it was mine. I wasn't even by him when he found it in the middle of the crowd. He said he didn't know, he just felt like it was mine. Telling that story to Stacey gave us both chills.

The other time was earlier in 2014. I kept the crucifix in my car on this perfect little ledge at the bottom of the GPS below the dash and above the stereo. The metal loop where a chain is supposed to go through, so you could wear it as a necklace, locked in perfectly between the cushion landing of the ledge and the frame of the GPS screen preventing it from sliding around while driving.

My car needed service work and it was going to be in the shop for a few days, so rather than tempt fate, I took it out of my car and placed it in the loaner vehicle at the dealership. When I got home I brought it in and put it in the cabinet where I keep all my stuff. That was Wednesday evening.

Now this part I remember perfectly. That Saturday was a darker, damp, cloudy and drizzly, but not rainy, day. The dealership called around noon to say the car was ready so I loaded up the crucifix and drove to the dealership. As I exited the vehicle to go pay and exchange their loaner for my car, I put it in my right front pocket. In the haste of trying to get out of the dealership quickly to get to the cleaners before they closed, I forgot to place it back on the ledge in my car and drove home where I reached in my pocket and it was gone.

My heart sank and I panicked. I went through my entire car, taking everything out from floor mats to every piece of paper, moving the seats forward and backward, getting a flashlight to double check, but it was nowhere to be found. I searched the house inside and out but to no avail. I called the dealership and had them check the loaner car — that was a negatory. I felt awful, I felt like crying and I actually did a bit. My stomach hurt, my mind was racing, playing every step I took over and over and over. I just couldn't find it, no matter how many times I looked in the car. Heck, I even looked in the trunk and I didn't even go in there.

Somewhere around 9:00 p.m. I gave up and came to the conclusion it was gone. I told this to Stacey and she tried to make me feel better by saying Cal didn't buy it and he really didn't have it long. Wasn't working, I vowed to keep that forever as a memory of Cal and it was gone.

Over the course of the next several days I did check and recheck. I retraced my steps and wracked my brain thinking about where it could be. It was gone and I just had to come to terms with it. I started Googling crucifixes to see if I could find an exact match but I could not. Nothing looked as cool as that one and it was gone.

On Thursday of that week I had gone to bed, but then I remembered I had to do something for work so I went downstairs to the closet in our office to get it. I opened the doors and right there in front of me in clear, open light on the top front edge of the filing cabinet with nothing hiding any part of it was the crucifix.

I was overcome with joy, disbelief, bewilderment, excitement and a hundred other emotions all at once, to the point all I could say out loud what was "WTF!?!" though I actually yelled out each word not just the first letter of each.

I wanted to run up and tell Stacey but she was sleeping so I did a little celebration dance on my own. All the while, I could not figure out how it got there and better yet, with all the people, including Stacey, who come in and out of the home office for Cal's Angels, how did no one see it. I know for a fact I was never in the office that Saturday but yet it disappeared and wound up in the office closet five days later.

The next day I told Stacey and she was extremely excited and asked me several times if I'm sure I never went in the closet. I know I wasn't and better yet, even if I did why would I take the crucifix out of my pocket and put it on the shelf? She summed it up nicely when she said, that before she fell in love with me she wished she knew that freaky things like this happen to me on a regular basis, she probably would have run. Not sure what it all means but I know there is a guardian angel looking over me and that I have a crucifix with a mind of its own.

The whole ordeal we endured with Cal and what has occurred since has also strengthened my faith in God. Knowing that Cal is in Heaven with God and Jesus, looking down on me and seeing all that I do is comforting. Knowing I will one day be reunited with my boy again gives me something to look forward to. It also allows me to accomplish all I set out to do by putting all of it in His hands and letting Him guide me.

It took losing my oldest child to wake my butt up and realize I am but just a mere conduit for God's work in Cal's Angels and in life — I now know why I am here on this earth. It is to be there for others first and help them with whatever it is they are struggling with — whether it be work, running a business, dealing with the loss of a loved one, winning at sports, getting through and succeeding through adversity or learning to love who you are and understanding your true definite purpose in life — I now know I have a role in this life to help everyone live life to the fullest, do all they can to harness their God-given talents and choose the right path when that fork in the road appears.

CHAPTER FIFTEEN TAKEAWAYS — DISCUSSION TOPICS

FAITH:

•   Define faith in your own words.

•   Can you reason with faith?

•   Is debating someone on religion and politics worth its while?

- Are friendships worth losing over debates on beliefs or opinions? Have you ever lost a friend over either your or their beliefs?

- Is it ever okay to force your thoughts and opinions on others? If so, when and why is it okay? If not, why not?

ACCEPTANCE:

- What helps or would help you come to terms with and accept the death of a loved one especially your child?

LEADERSHIP:

- Why do some who are not succeeding refuse to follow a tried and true method of doing what it is they are trying to succeed at?

- Discuss the saying, "You can't teach an old dog new tricks." Can you? Then add in the extra line, "But you can't teach a stupid dog old tricks either." What does this mean to you?

- Can a "me first" person be a great coach? Why? Why not?

- What makes a coach a great coach?

CHAPTER SIXTEEN
The Mind is a Powerful Thing

"With everything that has happened to you, you can either feel sorry for yourself or treat what has happened as a gift. Everything is either an opportunity to grow or an obstacle to keep you from growing. You get to choose."

Wayne W. Dyer
American Self-Help Author, Motivational Speaker

We speak different languages, practice different religions, look different, act different, smell different even react differently to common situations — we are all different but yet, at the same time, we really are all the same. More now than ever before it is so hard for me to figure out why we just cannot deal with these outward differences and all get along.

It is absolutely perplexing as to why we cannot all do this in concerted effort — it takes one to start but the rest to follow. I am willing to be the one to take the lead; I just need the rest of you to realize that at the core we're all the same … we all are human beings.

And while we're at it, let's all laugh about some of this too. Everybody needs to stop being so sensitive and laugh at themselves, laugh at me, laugh at their friends, laugh at each other with each other and get on with life … and while we're all laughing, let's always be cognizant of the fact that we're all in this world together.

Cal's mother gets bogged down in this, in the negativity, the blame game, the worst in everyone and everything. My only comments to her are, "Come on, Cal had cancer and he died from the complications relating to it not as a result of anything I did or didn't do."

There is nothing anybody did, could have done, did not do or wouldn't have done. Come to terms with the realities of the situation so that you can move on with your own life rather than remain stuck in the past. It is when you do this that you will finally find peace.

And this is not just advice for her — it is advice for everyone. The laws of sowing and reaping are real — try it out for yourself and you too can free yourself of many burdens of the mind, heart and soul.

There are people who legitimately cannot take care of themselves. I look at those whom we help through Cal's Angels. Whether it be financial assistance or a wish, there are people who need help in one way or another. Why don't others just step up and help? In my opinion, that is where you can get strength to just go out and look at the positive things in life and say I cannot only take care of myself but I can also help take care of others.

This is something for everyone to latch onto and look to the future saying, "I am alive, I am well, I am here and I can make a difference not only in my own life but in the lives of others who need me."

I know that all this "positivity" may sound hokey to some. There is no way everyone can wake up every single morning, look in the mirror and find something positive to start the day off on the right foot … but I sure try and I almost always succeed in doing so.

It makes life all that much more worth living — especially when you can reflect and add a moment to give thanks to God for everything that is good in your life rather than curse him for everything that is bad, wrong or "just not right."

There are many people who take negative situations, like a serious illness or accident, and turn it around. They work with awareness groups, accident prevention groups or support various related charitable organizations which gives them a true passion for their fellow human beings and life in general. Or they just do what my good friend Tom "Too Tall" Cunningham does.

Tom was diagnosed with Rheumatoid Arthritis at the age of five. In the next 45 years since then he has had four hips, four knees and two shoulders replaced and been hospitalized 40 times. His growth was stunted at 5'1" due to the heavy daily doses of the oral steroid Prednisone that he started taking as a young child to fight his arthritis.

Despite his physical challenges, Tom is well known for always answering "amazing" when asked how he is doing. If you ever want to be motivated and/or inspired to do something positive and forget about all of your problems, just call Tom and his extremely positive attitude will lift you out of any negative mood you're in. Truly inspirational!

The Earth is such a vast place but yet, at the same time, it really is a very small place. "They" say you are only a maximum of five degrees of separation from everyone else — within your closer circles there is someone who has experienced exactly what you have experienced or a lot more than you think who have experienced worse. Many of these people struggle with the same things we do but we don't realize it — we tend to think we're alone in our struggles — "Why me?" is the norm for the vast majority of us.

While at times it may not appear to be this way, I do struggle a lot with the loss of Cal. I try to be upbeat at all times not just for my own sanity but for those around me as well, but to say that I am truly upbeat all the time would be a lie. There are times I feel like giving up and saying, "I'm done and cannot do this anymore," asking myself, "Why do I struggle to be successful? Why do I put myself through the trouble to run Cal's Angels at such a high level? Why not just hang out and let others take care of me?"

There are also the very rare times the fleeting thought of giving up and bashing my head against a wall crosses my mind but what would that really accomplish? Nothing except to screw my life up which would adversely affect my family and those who depend upon me to succeed at the insurance gig and to keep Cal's Angels flourishing. No matter the reason for doing it, anyone purposely bashing their against the wall would certainly make it hard to be seen as normal and certainly not someone folks would want to buy insurance from or support via Cal's Angels.

Before I let me talk myself into being what Napoleon Hill refers to as a "drifter", I stop and take a good look at my life and me from all angles. I am able to get up feeling alive and refreshed every morning even if I only grab the usual five hours of Z's on weeknights, I am able to get in a good workout, get around freely, perform all daily duties unassisted and, best of all, meet new people on a regular basis.

Then combine with all these abilities I am blessed with the fact that there are a lot of good people in my life who depend on me including friends, colleagues and family which gives me such a great feeling that I come out of any "funky" mood I may be in at the moment.

When you wallow around in those negative feelings and are controlled by negative thoughts, no one wants to be around you. That doesn't mean just changing for five minutes and expecting things to be better right away. It takes time to build the necessary momentum to make it an active part of your life — to create a habit of positivity in your life. You almost need to schedule it and make it a formal part of your day. Start with five simple minutes then move to ten, fifteen, twenty and before you know it you are doing it on a regular basis all day long.

In your mind portray that image of who or what you want to be and eventually you will become it. Will this happen all the time? Every time? Of course not; no one can do that but I guarantee if you try it and try hard enough with the inner desire to want to do it for a sufficient period of time it will happen most of the time.

The mind is a powerful thing — just as it gets you into a negative state of mind, you can train it to bring you into a positive state of mind but it takes time, patience and determination to achieve it. I love another one of Napoleon Hill's quotes, as it is so true: "Whatever the mind can conceive and believe it can achieve," to which I want to add my own addendum: "But it ain't gonna be an easy road for some of us."

If you really boil it down, we are all products of the culmination of our life experiences. We all go through trials and tribulations — some good and some not so good. We have to resist using those bad experiences to justify why we cannot be the best we can be.

I firmly believe that people who blame their circumstances on their prior experiences either have not learned to take care of themselves or don't want to take care of themselves for whatever reason. They make excuses to be lazy, unhappy or unsuccessful and believe they have no other choice but to be in the state they're in for good — to be "stuck in a rut" with no way out … to be a "drifter." If this is you and you want to change, I mean truly want to change, the first step you need to take is to change this mindset and take care of yourself by:

- Eating right

- Exercising regularly

- Reading often

- Constantly learning new things

- Learning from your past failures, adversities, heartaches and sorrows

- Growing as a person

- Improving your mind, body and spirit

- Being thankful and grateful for all that you have that is good

People will always pick up on whatever you do, how you act, react and what you say — make sure it is all good.

When you can take care of yourself and be a positive person, you can convert almost — and I stress almost — any experience into a positive one. If you are unable to do this you will either be unfulfilled or unhappy and that will spill over into the rest of your life.

CHAPTER SIXTEEN TAKEAWAYS — DISCUSSION TOPICS

PEOPLE:
• Are we really all the same at the very core of our being?

• Why do you think it is we can't laugh at our differences, poke fun at each other, kid around and still get along?

BIG QUESTIONS:
• Why is it that someone would search for answers to something that has no answers like the reasons for a child dying from cancer?

• In your opinion, what are the laws of sowing and reaping?

• Explain the "five degrees of separation" rule in your own words. Do you believe it? Have you experienced it?

COPING:
• What stops you from going off the deep end — if it has ever happened, that is?

• How do you get rid of your negative thoughts, feelings or intentions?

CHAPTER SEVENTEEN
Taking Action

"Those who believe they can do something and those who believe they can't are both right."

Henry Ford
American Industrialist

The harsh reality is that there is so much in life that, in layman's terms, just plain ol' sucks. It is so easy to let all of this control your attitude taking over your entire life leading to the hopeless conclusion that your life is not all you want it to be and there is nothing you can do about it. But there is and it all starts with the control you have over your own mind and how you see things.

If there is anything in life that I can put my finger on as being the single most important thing you can do for yourself that will allow you to take care of everything life throws at you in stride, it is the ability to consistently practice positive self-talk (PST).

For many of us positive self-talk may seem to be a daunting task to tackle but, like anything else in life, it can be learned through the process of creativity and creating a habit of it and making it an automatic part of your persona.

I start my day 30 minutes earlier than I need to start it so that I can use the time to reflect on what has happened in my life leading up to the present, plan on what I want to accomplish for today and where I want to be professionally, spiritually, mentally, physically and emotionally in the future. I do not proceed with anything until I am able to give ample time to acknowledge all I am thankful for in my life:

- I'm alive.

- I am healthy.

- I have a lot of great people in my life.

- I have an awesome family especially a strong wife who loves and supports almost everything I do.

- I have a lot of great friends.

- I have nothing but opportunity ahead of me.

If you have more than three of these things going for you, life is good and you're on the right track. If you have fewer than three, appreciate what you have and build up the rest from there.

From experience, especially my own, I truly believe that 90% of the people who say their lives suck actually want them to suck. Of course, if you ask them they won't openly admit this as they don't overtly want them to suck but yet, covertly, they either consciously or subconsciously want their lives to suck.

It could be low self-esteem, the inability to overcome adversity, lack of desire to succeed, unwillingness to practice PST or something much deeper — for whatever reason or reasons they are self-directing their path to an unfulfilling life.

Many people will tell you they just cannot give up an extra 30 minutes of sleep — heck they swear they can't even give up an extra five or ten. I'm here to tell you that yes, you can but you have to work at it. Your mind is an incredible thing and you can do anything you truly believe you can do. Go to bed earlier and for every minute you go to bed earlier get up that much earlier. Start with five minutes until it becomes easy then go to ten, fifteen and so on.

Maybe you don't do thirty minutes — maybe twenty is enough. However much time you need to start your day right is up to you and will differ for each one of us. Trust me when I tell you that starting your day this way is great for the mind, body and soul no matter how long it takes you to have a positive outlook on life and believe you have a lot of good things going on in your life.

The biggest lie you can tell yourself is that, "I have nothing good in my life." There has to be at least one good thing and that is all you need to start. It may not even be a big thing, just something. Once you start to appreciate or understand that one thing, you'll start seeing more things — usually the little things you took for granted become clear. This will translate into more positive things as the days come and go, the weeks go by, the months pass and life goes on.

You will start to change and grow as a person. People want to be around others with good, positive attitudes and great demeanors.

As your attitude and behavior become more positive, you will experience better health and a better life. It's a snowball effect that will change your life and make you someone positive, someone successful people want to be around furthering the snowball effect. I am a firm believer in the saying that you are the average of the five people you spend the most time with. Negative people bring on negative feelings, emotions and attitudes — positive, successful people breed positive, successful attitudes and pleasing personalities that change lives for the better.

I'll say it again: "Get up and grab those extra five to ten minutes each morning. Don't tell me you can't because I know you can. Let me know if you need a wake-up call, Hotel Sutter is there to help you!"

The only way you can succeed at changing yourself is that you have to want to change, I mean really want to change and if you do you absolutely can start the snowball effect that will change your life forever.

I know how this works, both for the positive and negative, especially after losing Cal. In fact, there are days I still start in a very negative place. I may lose a big account at work, something terrible comes up in my life or happens to a dear friend or family member — whatever it may be, sometimes it is hard to get started because I just do not feel like doing anything. The whole "negativity thing" slides in and takes control.

It really is how you look at life and everything in it. You are never going to be positive all the time and I am sure not Mr. Positive Energy all the time nor am I the poster child for continuous positive energy. However, it is a cumulative effect that I am constantly working on for myself. I lost my boy, my first born, an excellent athlete when he was 13 and I have every reason to hate the world, God and, for no real reason at all, probably even you but I don't.

Just start your day by trying to smile. Simple, just smile about something like a pet, your children, your spouse, some funny photos or a great vacation. People want to be around others who smile — it's like a magnet for other positive happy people. How you start your day translates into how the rest of your day goes especially when the power of the Law of Attraction works its magic in a positive manner for you.

In the process of starting your day, be sure to take care of yourself. Everything from eating right to exercise to PST is essential because an unhealthy you cannot be the positive force you need to be to attract what is necessary for the snowball effect of positivity to occur. You need to constantly work on all of this and the good news is that you can.

I have also found that "getting involved" is extremely therapeutic for the mind body and soul. Involved in study groups, sports, church, committees — anywhere there is genuine human interaction taking place. In order for there to be "genuine human interaction" you need to be the sort of person that others want to interact with and have involved in these groups which brings us back to getting, maintaining and strengthening that positive upbeat attitude.

But even deeper than that, you have to sincerely want to get involved and stay engaged with whatever group it is you are in. In community — in charity work, especially charity work, the reason is pretty simple. When you do charity work, you have to put your own feelings, needs and desires aside, at least for a little while. Even if it is only once a week, give yourself up and give it to that charity in a wholehearted way ... you'll be glad you did and you can quote me on that!

As I stated earlier, I have two jobs: One that pays the bills and one that pays the heart. It is when you can truly say that you have a job that pays the heart and you are completely satisfied with that sort of payday for your efforts that things start to change.

This doesn't mean that you do not need to take care of yourself first; you do. But once you've done that, try giving yourself up to something else that can be of benefit to others — to a cause bigger than yourself and see what starts to happen to you as a person. Some people do this with their religion, with a charity or with their family.

That is all great, however, try stepping outside of your family to get a different perspective on things. To do it for complete strangers, people you have never met before, whose paths you may never cross again brings an extremely elevated level of fulfillment and satisfaction to all of this. The feeling of self-worth and affirmation of how you have done something for someone and the only thing you expect in return is to feel good about it is inexplicably exhilarating.

All of this charity work, volunteering and thinking about others first is something I never knew before Cal started his fight with cancer and something I never thought I would have given a second thought to until after we lost Cal. Anyone who knows me well knew my priorities.

It's not so much that my priorities have changed but I discovered my true definite purpose in life which automatically flipped my priorities in reverse order with me only listed once and it's after God and family. Now I do all of these great things for others and I love it. Even when I'm exhausted and can't go on I still look at what we've done with Cal's Angels and am overcome with a sense of complete satisfaction from all of it.

The feeling of complete satisfaction is bolstered by reading a letter from one of the families we've helped through Cal's Angels telling us how much it meant to them to have Cal's Angels in their life.

How the laptop we provided made it easier for their child to go through grueling cancer treatments, how we connected them to health and wellness resources and how we were able to provide mental and emotional support by connecting with them on a level field of "having been there" ourselves or with awesome wish granting families who have become lifelong friends. It is emotionally and spiritually uplifting to know that we were able to make their lives just a little more tolerable for at least a few hours if not forever.

It all starts with the core person you are. Some of the things you volunteer for may be unpleasant to you, but you have to ask yourself why they are unpleasant to you. Is it because they take you out of your comfort zone? Or perhaps you are uncomfortable doing something for nothing tangible in return.

These are some big questions but then, the payoff is even bigger. It certainly has changed my perspective on people. I have a much deeper understanding of people; what they do and why they do it. It has given me the ability to step back and read people pretty well with almost 100% accuracy.

Give me fifteen minutes of one-on-one time and I can tell you what makes them tick in business, relationships and as a friend.

Reading people is something that really cannot be taught. In order to have that in-depth perspective on people and who they really are at the core, one must have had a wide variety of life experiences that exposed them to a vast array of different people from every walk of life. I find it so fascinating and intriguing that in general, people fall into categories of similar behaviors based on certain traits, characteristics and mannerisms.

This whole journey has given me the confidence to know that I can handle pretty much anything. I know there is nothing worse than losing a child that can happen to me so I'm game for just about anything. It has gone so far as to bring me into public speaking; something I never wanted to do … at all, ever.

Funny, in a quirky kind of way, I'm a salesman and could always talk up a storm at a table in a small setting, but put me in front of a crowd and I thought I was going to puke. Now, at times, I crave it — it is exhilarating.

I also enter into relationships in far deeper ways I ever did before. I will welcome you into my circle until you prove to me you do not deserve to be there. I actually love being around people now, but just like the country song goes "you can take the cowboy out of the country but you can't take the country out of the cowboy," same holds true for my natural tendencies towards introversion.

You can get me to act like an extrovert but there are times I crave the energy I get from solitary, creative pursuits — the experts call it "Ambiversion" or being an Ambivert - moderately comfortable with groups and social interaction, but also relish time alone, away from the crowd.

Due to the nature of having six kids added to what I do with Cal's and the insurance business, "alone time" gets rarer and rarer but more often than not I absolutely enjoy my newfound open-arms stance which has allowed me to get on with life without forgetting where I have been and knowing where I am headed.

CHAPTER SEVENTEEN TAKEAWAYS — DISCUSSION TOPICS

- Discuss your interpretation of my statement, "There's a lot in life that sucks." Can people either consciously or subconsciously will their lives to "suck?"

LIFE:
- How do you start your day?

- What do you have to be thankful for in your life?

MIND:
- Discuss this statement and whether you believe it or not — "Your mind is an incredible thing and you can do anything you believe you can do."

- Do you feel like you have control over your mind? If so, why? If not, why not?

- Have you ever heard of Positive Self-Talk (PST)? Do you practice PST? When? Why? How? Is practicing PST easier said than done?

- Are you an introvert, an extrovert or an Ambivert? Which is better and why?

HABITS:

- Can habits change your life for the better?"

- In your opinion how are habits created?

- Can a person's priorities change?

- How do you have to "want it" to achieve it?

- How about negative people and/or negative personalities?

- What type of people do you attract?

- What type of people do you like to be around?

CHAPTER EIGHTEEN
How Do You Want to be Remembered?

*"If you would not be forgotten as soon as you are dead,
either write something worth reading
or do something worth writing."*

Benjamin Franklin
One of the Founding Fathers of the United States

Anybody can be a leader, can be excited, can be first in line when things are going great. The test is when you battle through tough times, when things aren't perfect ... where do you stand?

In 2011 we had our first team running for Cal's Angels in the Batavia Half Marathon. Everyone was getting on me to run it with them and I kept refusing by using every excuse in the book but they kept it up. Finally I said if we can get to 25 runners or more I will do it.

As luck would have it we hit that number and blew by it, so of course they were on me again, but I had seriously injured my right foot in April by getting my foot wedged up under the tread mill. Took nine stitches to close it up and three months to heal; I don't think they ever really did it right the first time.

I figured this was my ace in the hole as an excuse — foot in a boot until mid-July then we went to Minnesota for ten days. By the time I got back there was only a month to train so I was out for sure.

But no — one of our board members pulled out the trump card and pointed out that the race was on August 28th, the exact day Cal had passed away five years earlier. As Homer Simpson says, "D'oh!" All I could see was Cal calling me a little wussy boy with those little lips quivering in a puckered motion.

How could I say no? So I committed and started calling around to my running friends for a crash course in training for a 13.1 mile race.

They all concurred that this is not the ideal situation since I don't already run on a regular basis, but not terrible since I ride the bike and do the elliptical machines at the health club three or four days a week. I told them my goal is to run it without stopping — no record breaking attempts, just slow and steady all the way through without stopping. Not sure where the math on this makes sense but they said I need to go out right away and run six miles without stopping. If I could do that I can run 13.1 miles without stopping, but I needed to do the six miles three times per week leading up to the race, leaving three days before the race to rest with no running.

So that's what I did and while I made it those six miles, it plain ol' sucked. No other way to put it, just brutal stuff but I was bound and determined to do it. I pushed through the pain, the agony and even the boredom of running. It's very hard for me to concentrate for long stretches of time on the repetitive stuff that I really don't want to do in the first place. All I can say is, "Thank God for iPods and God Bless Steve Jobs!"

I can remember race day as it had so much meaning to me. My first long run, more than twice as far as I had ever run up to that date and the day my boy died five years earlier. I promised I would do this in his name as long as he watched out for me and carried me through to the end.

The race started early in the morning so I had to leave our house when it was still dark. On the way, I met up with at least half of the team at one of their houses and we all drove in a caravan arriving at the same time where we met the other 20+ runners. We stretched as a group and took photos as the sun started to rise.

As the runners started gathering by the start, the announcer called me up to the booth to say a few words about Cal's Angels. What an awesome way to start the race — great weather, sunny but yet cool for an August day, a great speech and PR opportunity and a great team to run with!

Start time came, the gun sounded and we were off. All I focused on was keeping it slow and steady, don't stop, think happy thoughts and listen to music that gets my blood pumping — a little bit of rock, some rap and sprinkle it with country — now that's a runner's mix for sure.

I won't bore you with a play by play but I'll tell you that when mile six came and went then mile seven and eight, I kept going and I started to feel really good about the chances of accomplishing my goal of finishing without stopping. My runner friends were right, but then the scare set in. Somewhere around mile ten my right hamstring went out but I did not stop. I hopped on my left foot while I pushed hard to kick out the pain.

As it was working its way out of my leg I was looking at the sky and talking to Cal. I said the same thing to him then as I did at our first 5k event I had to run just a few years earlier.

"You know I love you Cal, but this brutality is all your fault. I could be at home probably still sleeping or doing something a little more fun than torturing myself. Instead I am running 13.1 miles and raising money for kids suffering just like you did."

I said some more things that are just between him and me but the most important thing that comes of these talks is that it brings me right back to the whole reason for Cal's Angels itself. If Cal wouldn't have died, I wouldn't be doing what I'm doing and this little bit of pain I am experiencing is nothing compared to what these kids face during their battles with cancer.

Now I was getting to mile 11 and my hamstring went again, then yet again at mile 12, but I would not stop. I kept pushing through, just thinking about the pain I witnessed Cal enduring — it was horrible and excruciating

— I was not going to let it get the best of me. I was sweating and breathing hard while deep down there was a voice saying "give up, it's no big deal if you don't reach your goal, you gave it a good shot."

I refused and now I was in the clear. During that last mile both sides of the course were getting packed with more and more spectators as I got closer to the finish line. None of them knew me but they were still cheering me on. They were yelling words of encouragement and telling me to push on, don't give up.

With a half mile left I saw a group of people running the other way towards me and as they got closer I could see they were wearing Cal's Angels shirts. It was a group of about 10 runners who had already finished and decided to come back to run with me. To push me on and help me cross that finish line with all the extra energy and excitement you can only get from a show of unity like this. It was a thing of beauty, self-accomplishment and pride as I crossed the finish line. I did it, I ran a half marathon in 2 hours and 34 minutes — I did not stop nor did I waiver — I gave it all I had and I gave it for a worthy cause!

Go out and live every moment like it's the last play of the game, the last sale of your career, the last moment of your life because on that day at the end of your life when you look in the mirror and you know, you just know you gave it all you had and you gave it for a worthy cause. How do you want to go out — how do you want to be remembered?

None of what I have experienced in life — including cherishing then losing a son named Cal — was by chance. It all happened for a reason and I know with 100% clarity how I want to be remembered ... do you?

CHAPTER EIGHTEEN TAKEAWAYS — DISCUSSION TOPICS

- **Discuss and explain what this short but sweet chapter means to you.**

- **Where do you stand when times are tough, when things aren't going well?**

- **How do you want to be remembered? What are you doing to accomplish this goal?**

Please contact Tom at bookings@tomsutterspeaks.com for any of the following services:

- Speaking Engagements
- Risk Management and Insurance Protection Consulting for Businesses, Individuals and Non-Profits
- Non-Profit and For Profit Marketing and Branding Strategies
- Sales Training
- Establishing and/or Enhancing Corporate Give Back Programs
- Corporate and Non-Profit Employee, Board Member, Officer and Volunteer Recruiting Strategies
- Fundraising Ideas

10% of all proceeds from any of these services is donated to Cal's All-Star Angel Foundation to further assist families facing the battles of pediatric cancer.

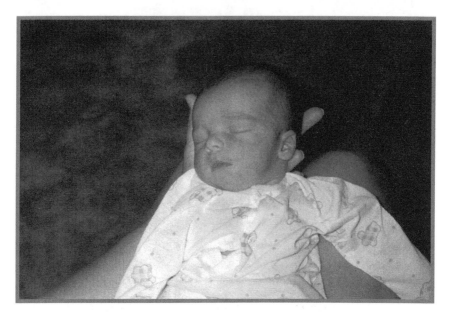

Baby Cal

Cal was a Sox fan before he knew how to be a Sox fan

Shortly before he was diagnosed, hanging with his brother Ryan

Tom, Cal and Ryan – The tough guys on wedding day

The new family on Tom and Stacey's wedding day

Just posing with two of our supporters

Doing Christmas in a tasteful Griswold fashion

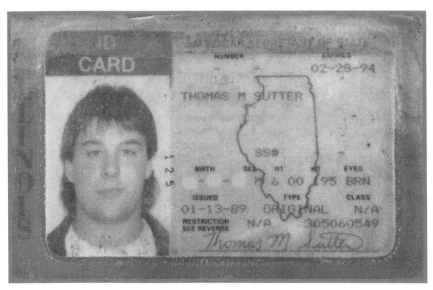

The rebel rouser in his heyday – Gotta' love the mullet

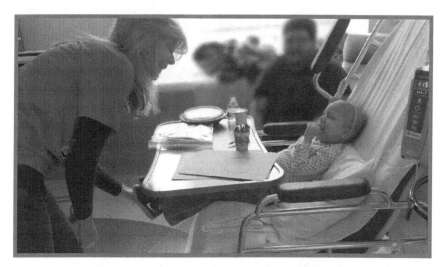

Stacey doing what she does best for the families
at Lurie Children's Hospital of Chicago

Lovin' the plaque showing our sponsorship
on one of the two floors at Lurie's!

*Scholarship winners at the game
when the two high schools played each other*

Second set of 8 Cal's Angels scholarship winners

*The Cal Sutter dedication plaque that was mounted
on the concession stand at St. Charles North High School's baseball fields*

The family stage at our 5K event

Having fun during the hard hat tour while Lurie's was under construction

Check presentation at our 5K event –
One of our wish recipients raised funds to help us continue our mission

Crossing the finish line after the grueling half marathon

The South Elgin Little League White Sox team Tom coached
that took 1st place on the Cal Sutter Field

Made in the USA
Middletown, DE
21 February 2015